Hindustani Music

A Study of its Development in Seventeenth and Eighteenth Centuries

AF673903

NAJMA PERVEEN AHMAD

Foreword by
DR. (MRS.) SUMATI MUTATKAR

MANOHAR
2026

First published 1984
Reprinted 2026

© Najma Perveen Ahmad, 1984

All rights reserved. No part of this publication may be reproduced or transmitted, in any form or by any means, without prior permission of the author and the publisher.

ISBN 978-93-88540-27-8

Published by
Ajay Kumar Jain *for*
Manohar Publishers & Distributors
4753/23 Ansari Road, Daryaganj
New Delhi 110 002

Printed at
Replika Press Pvt. Ltd.

To

Ustad Naseer Ahmad Khan Sahib
of Delhi Gharana

HINDUSTANI MUSIC

PREFACE

THE development of Hindustani Music goes back to the Vedic times and has been a continuous and un-interrupted process interwoven with the history of India. In this long time-span, the seventeenth and eighteenth centuries represent a unique period during which notable contributions were made to the styles and forms of music, and to musicology through books and manuscripts written in Persian and Urdu.

Whereas most of the heritage in Hindustani Music has been documented and studied in considerable detail from Sanskrit sources, surprisingly, the Persian and Urdu books and manuscripts on the subject remained relatively unexplored, causing a gap which has been noted by well-known musicologists like Pandit V.N. Bhatkhande. This work is a modest attempt to fill this void.

The book is divided into three sections: (i) Important manuscripts and books written during the seventeenth and eighteenth centuries (A.D.); (ii) Development of forms and styles during the period; and (iii) Musicians belonging to the period.

The first section has been devoted to the presentation and analysis of the major works, namely, *Raag Darpan*, *Tohfat-ul-Hind*, *Usulun-Naghmat-e-Asifi*, and eleven other manuscripts and books. These works provide information not only pertaining to the period during which they were written, but also about the development of music during approximately five hundred years before their time, because most of these are based on Sanskrit works of earlier and ancient *Shastras*. At the same time, the writers of these works have given equal importance to the state of art and theory of music as developed during their own period by giving comprehensive description of musicology and musicians during their time.

The second section has been devoted to a study of the origin and development of different styles of singing in the light of Persian and Urdu literatures and the major changes in such styles which occurred during the period. The study has exploded most commonly believed notions and myths about the origin of styles like Dhruvapad and Khayal, which have been generally considered innovations of a few individual personalities. It has been found that these have emerged over a long period of time from the earlier forms, in which major contributions were made during the Medieval period. The Persian literature of the period has given a very lucid picture of these developments, which had otherwise remained obscure. Similarly, one finds interesting clues regarding the development of forms like Qawwali, Tarana, Qaul, Qalbana, etc., which were developed as a result of the interaction of Indian music with external influences brought in by the Muslims from Arabic, Persian and other Middle East sources. The literature of the period has also brought to notice some of the unknown and obscure forms of music which are not traceable anywhere else, such as *Suraj Prakash* and *Chandra Prakash*.

In the last section of the book the classifications of musicians have been discussed, and description of the musicians belonging to the period has been given. This section brings to light interesting descriptions of the famous musicians of that time, their qualities, and their styles of singing.

This book is, therefore, an attempt to throw some light on the valuable contribution made to the development of Hindustani Music by Persian and Urdu literary heritage belonging to the seventeenth and eighteenth centuries. This literature, which has so far remained relatively inaccessible and mysterious to the musicologists, has been translated, described and critically analysed. The literature provides an important link in the continuity of the history of Hindustani Music from the ancient Sanskrit *Shastras* to the contemporary knowledge of musicology.

It is a modest beginning of the exploration of the rich treasure of knowledge in the field of music and fine arts contained in Persian and Urdu manuscripts and, hopefully, it will lead to further and more detailed studies of this literature in the future.

I wish to record my sincere and deeply felt gratitude to Dr-(Mrs.) Sumati Mutatkar, who provided me invaluable guidance, support and encouragement at every stage of my work. She has always been a source of inspiration to me as a teacher and scholar of music. I am also indebted to Professor S.A.H. Abidi, whose vast knowledge of Persian literature was a source of great help to me in this work. Mr. Mohammad Amin, well known teacher and scholar of Medieval Indian History at St. Stephen's College, Delhi, very kindly provided help and expert advice in surveying the historical perspective for this work.

I wish to especially mention my gratitude to Mr. Anees Chishti, without whose painstaking help and support this work could not have been published in this form. In a similar vein, I wish to acknowledge the most valuable help given by Mr. Rehmatullah Farooqi in translating many Persian books and manuscripts, for an accurate understanding of their contents.

NAJMA PERVEEN AHMAD

Faculty of Music and Fine Arts,
University of Delhi,
Delhi-110007
December 1983

CONTENTS

FOREWORD

I FEEL happy and privileged to place before the world of music this work of Dr. Najma Perveen Ahmad, entitled *Hindustani Music : A Study of its Development in Seventeenth and Eighteenth Centuries.* Based on her doctoral thesis, the book explores the musical panorama of the Seventeenth and Eighteenth Centurics (A.D.) in India, particularly with reference to the relevant works in Persian and Urdu manuscripts. The work keeps out mere generalities and highlights the demarcated field of enquiry thereby making it a concentrated and in-depth study.

For her study, Dr. Najma Perveen Ahmad has chosen three major works in Persian along with ten other Persian and Urdu books and manuscripts written during the period under review. For a proper scanning of the Persian manuscripts and books, expert guidance and help has been sought by her. The mainstay of this work is an interlacing of translation, description, analysis and critical observations on the valued works so studied. All the same, it is not an isolated amalgam. The findings have been linked up, correlated and presented in an integrated historical perspective.

The persent work is the first-ever endeavour to bring together so much fascinating and rich material drawn from primary sources, shedding light on a brimming and creative phase in the course of the development of Hindustani Music.

Pandit V.N. Bhatkhande, the great architect of modern Hindustani musicology, was well aware of the fact that several learned and informative works had been written in Persian during the medieval centuries which needed serious study and scrutiny. Drawing from these as much as he could, he had fully realised their importance. He had expressed his considered view that a complete perspective on the development of Hindustani Music would not be possible unless this lacuna is removed. The present work fulfils this long-felt need in a substantial manner. In fact, this could be viewed as the opening up of an avenue with a large vista leading to further investigations and insights.

I do hope that *Hindustani Music : A Study of its Development in Seventeenth and Eighteenth Centuries* by Dr. Najma Perveen Ahmad—her maiden venture in the field of musicological research—will receive a warm and encouraging welcome in the world of music and musicology.

DR. (MRS.) SUMATI MUTATKAR.

Introduction and Historical Background

THE origin of Indian music is shrouded in mysterious and fascinating legends associated with gods and goddesses, Rishis ane Munis, who were supposed to be the creators of music. Being one of the oldest civilizations, it is likely that music took birth in India much before it was developed in the other countries. One thing, however, is reasonably certain about Indian music—that it has been deeply associated with religious rituals, and probably it existed in its earliest form as hymns which were chanted in the rituals during Vedic times.

During its long journey through history, it has passed through several stages, and has been subjected to a host of external influences brought in by the invaders, inspite of which it has always maintained a profound continuity, consistency, and its own unique character and indentity. In fact, it has been like a mighty river, in which several streams have come and merged themselves, making it more rich, more colourful and more varied, and yet retaining its pristine beauty and grandeur. It has been like a powerful force, magnetic and enchanting, that attracted the kings and saints, the elite and the common man, the pundits and the mystics, all of whom fell in love with its charm, grace, and subtlety, and its capacity to inspire deep and sometimes ecstatic feelings.

Inspite of long periods of rule by the outsiders, Indian music never lost its vigour and popularity. Instead, it took into its fold the best of what they had to offer, and in the process it rejuvenated itself again and again. During the medieval period, when the Muslims came to India, once again Indian music went through a metamorphosis, blending in itself beautifully the Arab, Persian, and Central Asian influences, and gave brith to new forms and styles which continue to survive even today.

From the long history of Indian music which goes back to the Vedic times thousands of years ago, we have chosen for study in this work a short but significant span of two hundred years from the later medieval period, i.e., the seventeenth and eighteenth centuries, when the merger of Muslim influences was indistinguishable and complete, and had led to the emergence of some novel musical forms and styles. At this stage Hindustani music was most lively and vibrant, and it had engulfed all social strata and all walks of life. It had penetrated the royal courts as well as religious assemblies of the Sufi saints, the gatherings of the aristocrats and social functions of the people in general. Besides, in its devotional aspects, music continued to flourish in the temples, specially at the Vaishnavite temples.

The literature written on music during this period is also very rich and significant, as it gives clues not only to the theory, forms and styles prevalent during that period, but also to the profound wisdom and insights contained in the ancient Sanskrit Shastras which were studied by the authors and incorporated in their writings.

Historical Background : Medieval Period

Music continued to flourish in medieval India inspite of the acquisition of political power by the Turks, Afghans, and Mughals whose religion, in theory, appeared to frown on music that was meant for entertainment. It was patronised and it thrived at the imperial courts of Delhi and Agra, and at the centres of provincial kingdoms like the Sharqi kingdom of Jaunpur, Khilji kingdom of Malwa, the Bahmani kingdom, at Bijapur and Golkunda, and of course at the court of the Hindu Rajas and potentates. There was another aspect of music popularised by the Bhakti and sufi Saints besides the folk music. Their significance in the development of Hindustani music cannot be denied. If anything, it was more soulful and emerging entirely from the devotional and spiritual sources, which made it more profound.

The later medieval period, particularly the seventeenth and eighteenth centuries, forms a crucial period in the history of

India. It was during this period that the Mughal Empire in all its grandeur and glamour rose to its height, and then plunged down to decline and decay. The empire so ably founded by Akbar reached the peak of political and military greatness, and of cultural glory under Jahangir and Shahjahan. In the second half of the seventeenth century, under Aurangzeb's reign of religious orthodoxy, it began to decline visibly, and by the middle of the eighteenth century it came virtually to an end, though in a technical sense it continued to linger on till 1857 A.D.

The fluctuations in the fortunes of the Mughal Empire are not reflected in the same proportion in the domain of art and culture. During the period of its decline, architecture, painting and literature suffered only marginally in quality and excellence ; while music seems to have retained its vigour and vitality, and continued to enjoy popularity and patronage. This once more proves the contention that cultural fluorescence is not necessarily and exclusively dependent on material prosperity. It can transcend adversity and flourish in times of political instability and economic distress.

Mughal contribution to art and culture is well known. What is not so well appreciated is the intensity of their passion which is linked up with their earlier history, and the structure of the state that developed under them in India. The Mughals were the descendants of the Mongols who, owing to their pillage and plunder had acquired a notoriety as barbarians in India. The Mughals being conscious of this stigma made strenuous efforts to promote the finer arts in order to wipe out their earlier image and to project themselves as paragons of cultural refinement and urbanity. Probably this was the reason why they preferred to call themselves Chaghtais or Timurides, rather than Mughals. It was also through assimilation and promotion of the indigenous arts that they aimed to strike roots into the soil of the country and to found their government, if possible, on the willing consent and goodwill of the people instead of on brute force. "It is evident", says Beni Prasad, "that the Mughal State had risen from the level of a Law State or Police State to the rank of a Culture State".[1]

1. Prasad, Beni : History of Jahangir ; Allahabad, 1940, p.79.

A composite governing class and a composite culture were the twin pillars on which the Mughal state structure had been raised.

In every field of art there was intermingling of ideas and techniques, but the process of harmonious blending was so complete in music that any attempt to delienate the indigenous and the foreign elements would be an exercise in futility. The Hindustani music that developed during this time is essentially based on the rich Indian traditions and its interaction with the Persian, Arabic, and Central Asian influences. The contribution of the Mughals was primarily one of recognition, appreciation and patronage which helped in its popularity.

This work is primarily concerned with the seventeenth and eighteenth centuries. However, a brief survey of the popularity of music in the court as well as in the other sections of the society, and the interest taken by the Mughals in its promotion as described by the historians may be worthwile as a backdrop for this study.

Babur, though more interested in literature and horticulture did not neglect music. In his memoirs there are interesting descriptions of musical soirees and the excellence of the skill and performance of Indian musicians. The illustrations of Baburnama have a number of miniature paintings executed during the reign of Akbar.[1] These portray music being played on the battlefield,[2] in the court,[3] at wayside gatherings[4] and even on boats.[5] This indicates the popularity cf music during his time.

There is very little information about Humayun, but it does seem that in the section of nobility known as Ahl-e-Murad, musicians held high ranks along with poets. A long list of the names of musicians during his time is also available.[6]

1. There are two albums of these paintings: (1) Suleiman (ed) Miniatures of Baburnama, Tashkent, 1970; (2) S.J. Tyulayev, Miniatures of Baburnama, Moscow, 1960.

2. Suleiman, op. cit., Pl. 40 ; Tyulayev, op. cit. pls. 34,35.

3. Suleiman, op. cit., pl. 32

4. Ibid., pl. 45.

5. Ibid., pl. 94

6. Rizvi, Athar Abbas : Mughal Kaaleen Bharat, Aligarh, p. 292.

Akbar's reign has been immortalised by a number of great musicians like Tan Sen. Abul Fazl, no mean exponent of the art himself, goes into ecstacy while describing the charms of music. According to him the power of this 'talisman of knowledge' is supreme as it creates melodies which "move the heart to sorrow or joy" in accordance with the insight of the listener, and as such is of "immense use to those who have renounced the world and to such as still cling to it".[1] He tesitfies to the fond attention given by His Majesty to music and the patronage extended by him to those who "practise this enchanting art".[2] Almost a comprehensive list of all the famous musicians of the time is given. This includes such names as Miyan Tan Sen, Sujan Khan, Baba Ramdas, Baz Bahadur, Bilas Khan and Tantrang Khan, sons of Tan Sen, Surdas, son of Baba Ramdas, Rang Sen of Agra, Ustad Yusuf of Harat, Pirzada of Khorasan.[3] It appears as if the names have been arranged in order of merit. A large number of instrumentalists and the instruments in which they specialized are also mentioned.[4]

These musicians belonged to different religions and regions. "Hindus, Iranis, Turanis, Kashmiris, both men and women."[5] They came from diverse castes and social backgrounds. Love of music seems to have cut across the barriers of caste, social and professional classes.

Jahangir, though his love of music was not as pronounced as that of his father, continued the tradition. His memoirs and the Iqbalnama-e-Jahangiri mention the names of some prominent musicians. In the eleventh year of his reign he gave the title 'Anand Khan' to one Shauqi who sang "Hindi and Pesrsian songs in a manner that clears the rust from the heart".[6] Jahangir's interest in music may also be established

1. Ain-e-Akbari, (Eng. tr.), Blochmann and Jarrett, Calcutta, 1883. vol. I, p. 611.

2. Ain-e-Akbari, (Eng. tr.), Blochmann and Jarrett, Calcutta, 1883 vol I, p 612.

3. Ibid., pp. 612-13. (For details, see Section-C, Ch. VIII of the study).

4. Ibid., p. 613.

5. Ibid., p. 613.

6, Tuzuk-e-Jahangiri, (tr.) Alexander Rogers, Delhi (Reprint), 1968, p. 331.

from the fact that he used to listen to Ibrahim Adil Shah's compositions in music and appreciate them. The songs were sung by Bakhtar Khan Kalawant.[1]

Shahjahan's first love was architecture but music continued to receive royal attention. Among the musicians mentioned during his reign are Jagan Nath, Dirang Khan and Lal Khan, the son-in-law of Bilas Khan, the son of Tan Sen. Lal Khan was given the high sounding title Gunsamundar.[2]

The reign of Aurangzeb witnessed a general decline in cultural activities particularly in music which suffered a setback owing to his known hostility arising out of his religious orthodoxy and puritanical attitude. Performance of music, except of a devotional nature, was prohibited and "distinguished and well known musicians (Kalawantan and Qawwals) were asked to desist from music".[3] The anecdote about the funeral procession taken by the musicians to bury music and Aurangzeb's report, "Bury it so deep under the earth that no sound or echo of it may rise again" is so well documented that there is no reason to believe it to be concocted.[4] The popularity of the anecdote has tended to cloud the significance of the incident and has created an erroneous impression that it marked the demise of music during this period. The incident, on the other hand, reveals the intensity of the protest and the futility of Aurangzeb's attempt to ban music. According to Manucci, more than one thousand persons participated in the procession and as many as "twenty highly ornamental biers" were carried. He is quite categorical in his statement that Aurangzeb's order failed to prevent the nobles from listening to music.[5] This is also clearly borne out from the large number of musicians mentioned in various works for the reign

1. Ibid.

2. See f. n. 2 by Blochmann and Jarrett in Ain-e-Akbari, op. cit., p. 613 (Further details about these musicians are given in Ch. VIII).

3. According to Maasir-e-Alamgiri the order was issued in 1665. See Khafi Khan, Muntakhab-ue-Lubab, vol. II, p. 213; A. J. Syed, Aurangzeb in Muntakhab-ul-Lubab, Bombay, 1977, p. 245.

4. Khafi Khan, op. cit,, p. 211; Elliot and Dowson, History of India as Told by its Own Historians, vol, VII, p. 288; Noccolao Manucci, Storia Do Mogor (Tr.), William Irvine, London, 1907, Vol. III, p. 8.

5. Ibid., p. 8.

of Aurangzeb.[1] In fact, his reign records the largest number of works in music.[2] It is likely that having been prevented from performing, the lovers of music took to writing on music. It is generally believed that music reached the peak of excellence and popularity during the reign of the much maligned Muhammad Shah. It should be obvious that during less than fifteen years between the death of Aurangzeb (1707 A.D.) and the accession of Muhammad Shah (1719 A.D.) music could not have attained olympian heights, and shown such popularity as it did during this time if it had virtually died during Aurangzeb's reign. Music was too strongly rooted in the life and culture of India since ancient times to have been mortally affected by the imperial orders of a bigoted emperor, however powerful he might have been.

Music has always been an integral part of Hindu religion and rituals, and as such its popularity among them is natural and understandable. It is interesting to note that the charm and appeal of Indian music had attracted not only the imperial court, but it had also become an essential feature of the daily routine of life among the Muslims at all levels. Kings and Princes, the Umara and Mansabdars, and even the common folks of both sexes fell in love with it. Taking the cue from the Emperors, the nobles also welcomed musicians to their own courts, which in turn beecame the centres of dissemination of this wonderful art. The social status they enjoyed and the handsome rewards and remunerations they received gave a tremendous impetus to music. The high esteem in which Akbar held musicians and the honours that he conferred upon them is well known. Jahangir also did not lag behind. On the eleventh anniversary of his accession to the throne, he ordered that "whatever offerings were made (on that day) by anyone in the shape of 'cash or goods' was to be given away to the musicians by way of reward"[3] Shahjahan had Jagan Nath and Dirang Khan weighed against silver which was given over to them as present.[4] The patronage of musicians by

1. See Raag Darpan of Faqueerullah, pp. 90-102.
2. Ansari, N.H : Farsi Adab ba ahd-e-Aurangzeb, Delhi, 1969, pp. 451-60.
3. Tuzuk-e-Jahangiri, op. cit., p. 317.
4. f. n. 2 by Blochmann and Jarrett in Ain-e-Akbari, op. cit., p. 613; also J. N. Sarkar, Anecdotes of Aurangzeb, pp. 173-74.

nobles like Abdur Rahim Khan-e-Khanan has become legendary. Islam Khan, a noble under Jahangir who was known for his austerity (he wore only khadi and ate bread made of maize and saag) spent more than eighty thousand rupees a month on musicians.[1] Nobles vied with each other to secure the services of renowned musicians. This phenomenal increase in demand helped in improving the social status and the economic lot of the musicians. Music became a coveted, respected and a remunerative profession.

It was in those days probably the most effective instrument of social change. A man from the lowest caste and the poorest family could be accepted at par with the grandees of the empire and earn a fortune if he had the requisite skill. No wonder there was a profusion of musicians. The sudden rise in their number also smacked of opportunism and a mercenary attitude among some of them. Music to an extent was alienated from the serene atmosphere of solitude and meditation, and was brought into the affluent din and bustle of the court in metropolitan cities. To please the patrons in the hope of reward, and not so much the fulfilment of the creative urge, became the object of performance. In some cases, they became famous not so much because of the excellence of their skill, as by the prestige of the court with which they were associated and the money they earned. Still there were some noble souls who defied the power of the kings and resisted the lure of the court, and continued to sing for their own satisfaction. Popular lore is full of such incidents.

Soon musical knowledge and skill became the hallmark of culture. The highest in the land, even the Emperors, did not feel inhibited in singing themselves. Muhammad Shah Rangeela's public performances are too well known to be described. Apart from the great fascination for music among men, its popularity among women is also noteworthy. This was true both for the Queens and the princesses, as well as women of humbler status. Manucci has given the names of thirty three superintendents of singers in the female section of the court alone.[2] Each superintendent had ten apprentices.

1. See Maasir-ul-Umara, cit. in Salik, A. M: Muslim Saqafat, p. 419.
2. Manucci, op. cit., vol. III, p. 336.

and "each queen, princess, even concubines had their own sets of musicians".[1] This can give some idea of the size of musicians employed at the court and also the keen desire of the inmates of the palace not to be left lagging behind the men in their interest in and patronage of music. The names given to these exponents of the fine art are also of considerable significance. According to Manucci, most of them were Muslims but were given Hindu names like Sundar Bai, Lal Bai, Hira Bai, Ras Bai, Gyan Bai, Akas Bai, Kesar Bai, Mrignain, etc., names which are common among singers even now.[2]

Downton, in the account of his travels in India during the reign of Jahangir, was struck by the popularity of music among women of the imperial household. He observes, "Their women, their wives and concubines sing most melodiously, with such elevated and shrill voices, strained into the highest, yet sweet and tunable, rising and falling according to their art and skill, that I have been ravisht...with sweet achee"...[3]

Another major nucleus for musical performances and the development of music was the Dargahs of sufi saints where regular musical gatherings used to be held. There were many such Dargahs in north India, and a vivid description of musical sittings held there is given by Nawab Dargah Quli Khan of Hyderabad who visited Delhi in 1738 A.D. In his book, 'Muraqqa-e-Dehli,' he has given a detailed and lively description of the style of life and opulence in Delhi. According to him, regular and intense musical sittings were held at the Mazars (tombs) of Sufis, like Hazrat Bakhtiar Kaki, Shaikh Nizamuddin Chishti, Hazrat Amir Khusrau, Hazrat Naseer-Uddin Chiragh Dehli, Hazrat Shah Hasan Rasool Numa, Shah Aziz-Ullah, and Meer Ashraf, etc. He has also stated that Sufis who were living at that time, such as Shah Alam, Majnoo Nanak Shahi, Shah Kamal, Shah Ghulam Mohammad, Shah Rahmat-Ullah, and many others like them, used to hold forceful musical sittings in which large numbers of musicians

1. Ibid., p. 336.
2. Ibid., p. 336.
3. See M. Foster, Early Travellers in India, p. 144; also M. A. Ansari, European Travellers under the Mughals, Delhi, 1975; Nicholas Downton travelled in India during 1608-1615.

used to participate. He has given a very interesting and detailed account of the various famous musicians of Delhi at that time, as well as a description of the pervasiveness of music in all walks of life. Daily musical performances in gardens, dargahs, houses of aristocrats and musicians, etc., particularly during Basant used to be held, and it has been said that the number of singers, qawwals, mimics, and other performers was so large that it was almost impossible to count them.[1]

The charm of indian music was so great that not only the sufis, the kings, nobles of the imperial household but even theologians (Ulema) were attracted by this enchanting art inspite of their religious orthodoxy. Not only Faizi and Abul Fazl who were enlightened liberal scholars, their father, Shaikh Mubarak and even the bigot and the severest critic of Akbar's policy of Sulh-e-Kul, Mulla Badayuni, were lovers of music. Others who fall in this category are : Mulla Abd-us-Salam Lahori, Shaikh Maali, Shafi Yazdi, Shaikh Alauddin, Shaikh Jamali, and Shaikh Gadai, who at one time held the office of Sadr-us-Sudur (head of the religious and ecclesiastical department) were well known exponents of music.[2] Mulla Ishaq Dhari, Shaikh Dewan Dhari and Makhdum Bahauddin were some other notable religious leaders who excelled themselves at music.

There cannot be any more impressive evidence of the popularity of Indian music which seems ro have brought together in its fold, Hindus and Muslims, Sufis and Ulema, saints and sultans, rich and poor, in fact, men and women from different castes and social statuses. Music, therefore, functioned not only as an esoteric art, or a source of entertainment, but also as a powerful instrument of cultural integration and social harmony.

Side by side with the popularity and development of Hindustani music in the courts and dargahs, the devotional aspect of music was flourishing in the temples. In the famous Vaishnavite temples of Nathdwara, Vishnupur, Dwarika, Jagannath Puri, Mathura, Vrindavan, etc. the ancient musical traditions were vigorously maintained. It was at these temples

1. See Nizami, K. H: Purani Dilli Ke Halaat.
2. Ain-e-Akbari, tr. Blochmann, Vol. I. p. 612

that the fundamental continuity of the ancient devotional music and its rich traditions were preserved, and it was further nurtured and developed.

Since the knowledge and patronage of music was considered the hallmark of a cultured person, it became necessary for people to obtain books on music in the Persian language, which was the language of the court and upper classes at that time. There was a rich treasure of classics on Indian music available in Sanskrit language at that time which such people could not read or understand. Hence, a need arose to translate the Sanskrit books into Persian, and also to write books on music according to the contemporary state of art. Such literature was, therefore, produced in the Persian language, and the seventeenth and eighteenth centuries were especially rich in this respect. Apart form educating the readers about the various aspects of music, the writers, during this time, were also motivated by the spirit to preserve the rich heritage of Indian music as contained in the Sanskrit Shastras, and to make it available to the future generations of musicians and musicologists.

The earliest known Persian writings on Indian music are Ghunyat-ul-Munya (1374 A. D.); and Lahjat-e-Sikandar Shahi—a monumental work belonging to the Lodi period (1414-1526 A.D.). Emperor Akbar (1556-16C5 A.D.) had made the diognosis that the main reason for hostility between the Hindus and the Muslims was their ignorance about each other's religoin and culture. Therefore, under his instructions a large number of translations were undertaken of works, both religious and secular. Abul Fazl himself made an attempt in his Ain-e-Akbari to make a profound as well as popular study of the Hindu religion, philosphy, customs and manners. The whole of the third volume of this work is devoted to this subject. A full chapter deals with Sangeet. It is not an original study, and is largely based on the existing Sanskrit literature and discussions with the Pundits and scholars of the time. Still it does show a remarkable understanding of the fundamentals of the theory and practice of Indian music and is the result of prolonged and painstaking effort.[1] The inclusion of a full chapter on Sangeet in an official work commissioned by the Emperor himself gave tremendous prestige to the study of music and encouraged others to deal more adequately with the subject, which continued during the later period also.

This is evident from the fact that even under the regime of an emperor like Aurangzeb the academic interest in the subject was maintained, and a large number of standard works on music, both original and in translations from Sanskrit, were undertaken. A brief reference to some of them here may be illuminating. The detailed study of some of the major works of the period would be found in the later chapters.

Mirza Raushan Zamir who was well versed in Arabic, Persian and Hindi translated Parijatak, the classical work on music by Ahubal.[2] It is not a mere translation. Mirza Raushan Zamir has added his own comments also. The other famous work written during this persod is Raag Darpan by Saifuddin Mahmud Amir Faqueerullah. It is based on Mansingh Tanwar's Man Kautuhal.[3] Faqueerullah used most of the existing works on the subject, some of which are extinct now, and he has written a standard and comprehensive work on all aspects of Indian music. Qazi Hasan bin Khwaja Tahir bin Khwaja Muhammad was a prolific writer on music, who contributed significantly to the enrichment of musical literature. Three of his works: (1) Surud-ul-Bahr,[4] (2) Misbah-us-Surur,[5] and (3) Miftah-us-Surur[6] can be found today. The last one is probably a revised and expanded version of the second one. The comments of the author are significant. He admits that music as a form of entertainment is prohibited by Islamic law, but says that the natural desire

1. Ain-e-Akbari, (tr.) Jarrett, vol. III, Calcutta. 1887 pp. 245-257.

2. The Persian text is in the library of Aligarh Muslim University. The Sanskrit text with Hindi translation has been published from Hathras under the title, Sangit Parijat, in 1941.

3. For a detailed discussion, see Chapter I.

4. Written in 1562-63 A.D., Ms. in Salar Jang Collection, No, 1417-18, cit. in N.H. Ansari, op. cit., f.n. 3, p. 459.

5. Ms. in Asiatic Society, Calcutta, dated by the author, 1663 A.D,

6. Completed in 1673-74, Ms. in Bodleian, No. 3/3846, cit., in Ansari, op. cit., f.n. 2, p. 458.

of the heart overpowers the religious injunction. According to him, when God ordered the soul to enter the human body, the souls refused to do so. Then the angels were asked to sing, and it was the effect of their heavenly melody that induced the souls to enter the body.[1]

There is another work named Maarafat-un-Naghm by Abul Hasan Qaiser. Shams-ul-Aswat is yet another translation of a Hindi work by Ras Baras, son of Khushal Khan Kalawant. Tarikh-ul-Mousiqi and Risala-e-Mousiqi can also be cited as notable works of the eighteenth century. Two major manuscripts belonging to this century are Tohfat-ul-Hind and Usulun-Naghmat-e-Asifi. Both of these have been discussed in detail in Chapters II and III.

The works cited above clearly show that even during the period of Aurangzeb when music was supposed to have gone out of favour, musicians continued to practise their art, and the academic study of the subject attained new heights.

The foregoing discussion of the Mughal period clearly indicates that music received great patronage from most of the Mughal emperors, and it was highly popular in all segments of society. During this period, the Hindustani music assimilated many new influences brought in by the Arab, Persian and Central Asian sources, which led to emergence of new forms and styles. A great deal of literature was written in Sanskrit and Persian languages, and some books were also written in Urdu language in this period, particularly during the seventeenth and eighteenth centuries. These two centuries, therefore, have a special significance in the history of Hindustani music, specially from the point of view of the understanding of new influences on it during this period, and the record of the same in Persian and Urdu literatures.

Purpose, and Scope of Study

The purpose of this study is to take a close look at the development of Hindustani music during the seventeenth and eighteenth centuries, in the light of the Persian and Urdu manuscripts and books which have not been examined and studied as thouroghly as the manuscripts written in other

1. Ansari, op.cit., p. 458.

languages during the same period. Perhaps the reason for this gap is that the scholars of Persian and Urdu were rarely familiar with music, and the performing musicians were seldom concerned about the theory of music and its writing. As far as the modern Indian musicologists are concerned, they did realize the importance and need of studying the Persian and Urdu manuscripts on music. For example, Pandit V.N. Bhatkande, who was one of the most outstanding Indian musicologists, has repeatedly referred in his works to the need for examining Persian literature on Hindustani music. However, most of the modern Indian musicologists were not familiar with the Persian language and consequently they could not study such literature inspite of their desire to do so.

The study is a modest attempt to fill this gap in the literature of Hindustani music through translation, description, analysis, and critical commentary on the important Persian and Urdu manuscripts and books written during the seventeenth and eighteenth centuries. The three major works belonging to this period, namely, Raag Darpan, Tohfat-ul-Hind and Usulun-Naghmat-e-Asifi have often been mentioned in the literature on Hindustani music, with a cursory reference to their contents. These manuscripts have been chosen for detailed description and analysis along with the translation of important passages from them. In addition, Nadirat-e-Shahi and ten other books and manuscripts pertaining to this period have also been examined.

Based on the study of these manuscripts and books the development of various forms and styles of music has been discussed in the second part of the study. An intensive study has been made of the origin and development of Dhruvapad and Khayal, and other forms prevalent during the seventeenth and eighteenth centuries. An attempt has been made to identify the innovations, modifications, improvisations, combinations, and other changes introduced during this period in the basic forms of music, as well as the creation of new forms and styles. Several myths and commonly held notions about the development of forms like Dhruvapad, Khayal, Tarana, etc. have been critically examined in the light of the literature belonging to this period.

In addition to the major forms like Dhruvapad and Khayal,

a study has also been made of Tarana, Qawwali, Qaul, Qalbana, Naqsh-Gul, Naqsh-Nigar, Sohela and several other forms which were in vogue during the seventeenth and eighteenth centuries, as described in the manuscripts of that period.

Apart from the study of the theory of music based on the literature and analysis of the forms and styles of music, considerable material has been found about the musicians and their musical skill, which has been utilized for discussion in the last part of the study. The last chapter throws light on the status of the musicians in the courts as well as in the society at that time, their unique styles and methods of performance, and gives a vivid understanding of the rich and varied musical traditions during that period.

SECTION A

Important Manuscripts and Books of the Seventeenth and Eighteenth Centuries on Hindustani Music

THE most important source for studying the development of music during any particular historical era is obviously the description of music as given in the literature produced during that time. As discussed earlier in the introduction of the study, fortunately the seventeenth and eighteenth centuries witnessed an upsurge of writings on music which provides valuable information and insight into the forms and styles of music; the evolution, development and innovation of Ragas; names and description of musicians; the cultural and aesthetic tastes of people of the time; analytical and critical discussions on theory and history of music; and vivid descriptions of socio-cultural setting within which music was performed at that time.

During the seventeenth and eighteenth centuries a number of books on music in Sanskrit were written, which are very well known for their outstanding contribution to the understanding of the theory and practice of music. A few examples of some such well known books are the following :

1. Hridaya Kautuk, 2. Hridaya Prakash by Hriday Narain Dev (1660 A.D.): 3. Sangeet Parijat by Pt. Ahobal (later half of seventeenth century); 4. Rag Tatva Vibodh by Pt. Srinivas (first half of eighteenth century); 5. Sadraga-Chandradaya; 6. Ragmala; 7. Rag Manjari (all by Pundrik Vitthal (1600 A.D.)); 8. Anup Sangeet Vilas; 9. Anup Sangeet Ratnakar; 10. Anupankush (all by Bhavbhatt (end of eighteenth century)).

The above mentioned books have been discussed by many modern musicologists and some of these books have also been published and translated. As such the contents of these books are well known and have been utilised in understanding the development of the theory of Hindustani musical system. On the other hand, a number of other Persian and Urdu manuscripts belonging to the same period have often been mentioned, but these have not been studied in so much depth, probably because their translations were not available. Another reason for this gap might be that the scholars of Persian and Urdu were rarely familiar with music, and the performing musicians were seldom concerned about the theory of music and its writings. A modest attempt is being made in this thesis to fill this gap.

It may be mentioned here that several standard works in Persian were written even before the seventeenth and eighteenth centuries. Two of such works are : Lahjat-e-Sikandar Shahi, which is a monumental work of the period of Sikandar Lodi and Ghunyat-ul-Munya (1374-75 A.D.).[1] Ghunyat-ul-Munya, or the pleasure of desire, is the earliest Persian manuscript found on Indian music. The only copy of this work is known to exist in the India Office, London. This manuscript was found by Mrs. Khursheed N. Hasan, who introduced it through a paper which she presented to the XXIV Session of Indian History Congress, Delhi, 1961. The name of the author is not known.[2] This book provides valuable information about the development of various aspects of Indian music.

From the rich collection of books and manuscripts, the following three prominent manuscripts belonging to seventeenth and eighteenth centuries have been chosen for detailed analysis :

1. Raag Darpan

1. According to the catalogue of the India Office Library on Persian Manuscripts, Ghunyat-ul-Munya (richness of desire) was compiled by an anonymous author in the reign of Sultan Feroze Shah Tughlaq (1351-1388 A.D.).

2. Shahab Sarmadee : Ghunyat-ul-Munya ; Preface, Asia Publishing House, 1978.

2. Tohfat-ul-Hind
3. Usulun-Naghmat-e-Asifi

In addition, out of the remaining literature, Nadirat-e-Shahi and ten other manuscripts and books have been discussed in a summarized form.

The abovementioned three manuscripts have been chosen for detailed analysis, because their authors have taken into account our ancient shastric texts, and they have discussed all the aspects of Indian musical system. For example, the author of Raag Darpan has clearly stated that his book was translated from an old Sanskrit work entitled Man Kautuhal, in which he had incorporated his own viewpoints and a description of music and musicians of his time.

The writer of Tohfat-ul-Hind has also referred to the four classic books, viz., Sangeet Darpan, Man Kautuhal, Sabha Vinod, and Ragarnav, which he consulted for writing his book. Since these classic books are no more available, Tohfat-ul-Hind is an important source for the understanding of the rich knowledge contained in these books.

Similarly, Usulun-Naghmat-e-Asifi, which throws light on the later part of the eighteenth century, and which has been discussed at great length in several contemporary books, but the original text of which has been seldom brought to light, has been chosen for careful study and analysis. Major portions of the manuscript have been presented to enable a closer look at its contents.

The above selection of three major manuscripts along with ten other books and manuscripts in Persian and Urdu languages represents a cross-section of literature on theory of music, translations from Sanskrit books into Persian, biographies of musicians, musical compositions, and commentaries belonging to the period under study.

In the following chapters the abovementioned manuscripts and books have been presented in the form of a summary of the work, along with details about their authors and scribes, dates and context of writing, sources where these are available, translation of relevant passages, and critical commentary on the manuscripts.

CHAPTER I

Raag Darpan

RAAG DARPAN is one of the monumental works which were written during the seventeenth century. This manuscript was written during Aurangzeb's time. The manuscripts of Raag Darpan are available in several libraries of North India, such as, Reza Library at Rampur, Marris College Library at Lucknow, Maulana Azad Library of Aligarh Muslim University, and Dr. Zakir Husain Library of Jamia Millia at Delhi.

Three copies of this manuscript are available at the Maulana Azad Library, Aligarh Muslim University. In one of the manuscripts the year 1076 A.H. (1665 A.D.) is stated as the date of its writing, and it has been mentioned that this is the translation of Man Kautuhal. On the other manuscript the year of writing is the same, and it is stated that it was composed by Faqueerullah during his stay in Kashmir. On the third manuscript the name of the scribe is given as Mohammad Ahsan. However, in this manuscript there is a difference in the text after the second chapter.

Although several manuscripts were examined as part of this work, the manuscript at Jamia Millia was selected for the detailed study given here. This is a very well preserved manuscript. It is written on a very fine white paper, and the script can be read clearly except for a few paragraphs. This manuscript was earlier kept in a high school library, Moradabad, a district in U.P. There are three stamp markings on the front and one on the back of the book. One stamp is of a high school library, Moradabad and the other three stamps are in Persian which are not very clear.

A comparison of the manuscripts available at various libraries stated above gives an impression that the manuscript available at Jamia Millia may be the original manuscript. This inference is supported by the facts that the quality of paper of this manuscript is relatively much superior than the other manuscripts, and the seals on it indicate the period of Mohammad Shah. Another possible inference can be that this manuscript was one of the better copies, which was kept in the library of an Amir during Mohammad Shah's period, because in the seals on the manuscript the name Mohammad Shah is legible. The date mentioned in this manuscript is 1076 A.H. (1662-63 A.D.) and the writer's name is given as Amir Faqueerullah Saif Khan.

Amir Faqueerullah's father, Tarbiat Khan, was a courtier during Shahjahan's reign. Faqueerullah also joined the royal service during Shahjahan's reign. After Aurangzeb's ascendance to the throne, Faqueerullah proved to be a very courageous person who fought several wars. Aurangzab was very pleased by his achievements and awarded him the title of Saif Khan. Saif Khan progressed rapidly, and was made governor of several states from time to time, such as Kashmir, Allahabad and Multan. But he was relieved from his position as a governor twice when the emperor was unhappy with him. Faqueerullah himself has stated in his book : "I started writing this book in A.H. 1071. In A.H. 1073 I was again invited by the emperor. At that time I accompanied him to Kashmir. Although the emperor rarely took anybody along with him on such journeys, I was very fortunate to be chosen to accompany him to Kashmir".[1]

A perusal of Raag Darpan reveals that Faqueerullah was a patron of the musicians and was himself highly knowledgeable in the subject of music.[2] He has stated that he composed several Raags. He has also given names of the Raags composed by him which will be described later.

Raag Darpan is basically a translation and commentary on

1. Faqueerullah : Raag Darpan; p. 107.
2. Faqueerullah : Raag Darpan; pp. 89-90.

the earlier book Man Kautuhal, which was written during the period of Raja Mansingh Tanwar of Gwalior (1486-1518 A.D.).

Faqueerullah has given details in the first chapter about the book Man Kautuhal, and his own description, which may be summarised as follows :

"To those who are fond of music, Faqueerullah says that he found an old manuscript, Man Kautuhal. This book was written during the rule of Raja Mansingh, who was the King of Gwalior and was a great patron of music. He had a vast knowledge of this art. He composed Dhrupad style of music. He discussed and debated the subject of music with some renowned musicians of his time. Following are some of the names of such musicians :

"Nayak Bhannu, Nayak Bakshoo, Nayak Pandvi of Telengana, Mahmood, Lohang, Karna.

"When above experts were assembled in Gwalior, the King felt that it was very rare for so many Nayaks to assemble together. He, therefore, considered it desirable that the views of different musicians about the various ragas be discussed and the same may be recorded in writing so that posterity may be benefited from such writings. Consequently, all the performers and scholars of music discussed the various Raags, Raginis and their Putras, and compiled a book on music, in the name of Raja Mansingh. This book was named 'Man Kautuhal'. Since such a book could be considered a reliable and authoritative source, I have chosen to translate it. I have prepared a brief version of Man Kautuhal and named it Raag Darpan (Mirror of Melody). Raag Darpan would eliminate the need for going through Bharat Sangeet, Sangeet Darpana, and Sangeet Ratnakar".[1]

For preparation of this book Faqueerullah had consulted the following books :

(1) Nritya Nirnaya (2) Risala Syed Mansoor (3) Raag Prakash (4) Chandravati.

Nritya Nirnaya and Chandravati contain the details of

1. Faqueerullah : Raag Darpan; p. 34.

Raags and the timing of their singing, and Faqueerullah has written Raag Darpan mainly on the basis of these two books.[1]

Faqueerullah has mentioned that another book entitled Raag Sagar was written during the period of Emperor Akbar. About this book he has noted with surprise that the descriptions of Raags given in this book do not tally with the descriptions given in Man Kautuhal. It may be noted here that these two works could be considered contemporary works. Faqueerullah did not choose to translate Raag Sagar because most of the musicians in Akbar's court were Atai (merely performing artistes), and not scholars of music. Some of the names of such musicians are as follows :

(1) Sujan Khan Nahar (2) Sur Gyan Khan Fatehpuri (3) Chand Khan (4) Suraj Khan (5) Mian Chand (6) Baz Bahadur of Malwa.

Faqueerullah has also mentioned the names of Bakshu, Pandvi and Bhannu, whom he considered renowned Nayaks of Raja Mansingh's court and according to him none of the musicians during Akbar's time could match them.

Faqueerullah further writes :

"According to the earlier traditions, the vocalists used to be seated in the front and their accompanists used to be seated on the back side. The musicians used to study books on music and also used to discuss and debate the subject of sangeet shastra. But these days musicians have started performing without acquiring knowledge about it. As a result, the standard of music has gone down. That is why such musicians are called Pandits instead of being called Nayaks. These reasons prompted me to translate Man Kautuhal in preference over Raag Sagar".[2]

In the chapter on Raag Raginis, Faqueerullah has stated that in addition to the liberal translation of certain books he has also added his own understanding about the various aspects of music, about which he has asked the readers to indicate if they find any deficiencies. At various places he has also given an account of various significant historical events.

1. Faqueerullah : Raag Darpan, pp. 3-4.
2. Faqueerullah : Raag Darpan p. 15.

For example he has narrated his experience of his arrival in Delhi in the chapter on Khyal in the following words :

"We have returned to Shahjahanabad. It is built adjacent to Delhi. All the famous musicians who were in Agra earlier have shifted to Shahjahanabad. On one side of this city there is Jahanuma, and its southern part merges into Delhi. Its gardens and canals are beautiful beyond description".[1]

After this a number of couplets in praise of Shahjahanabad have been written. On the same pattern he has described some events which took place during his stay in Kashmir.

It seems that Faqueerullah wrote this work to present it to Aurangzeb, because he wanted to please him. But it appears that he could not succeed and he could not receive the royal appreciation and patronage for his work.

Raag Darpan is based on the following ten chapters :

1. Rationale for writting Raag Darpan. 2. Description of Raags. 3. Season and time for performing various Raags and auspicious and inauspicious words in Dhruvapad and Khayal singing and description of Gram. 4. Description of Svaras and different forms of Hindustani music. 5. Classification of instruments, categories of Nayaks and Nayikas. 6. The qualities and defects of musicians. 7. Description of different types of voice. 8. Description of Vaggeykara (composer) and classification of vocalists. 9. Description of Vrind (orchestra.) 10. Description of contemporary musicians and musical instruments.

In the first chapter, as stated earlier, the author has described the reason for selecting Man Kautuhal for translation in preference over other known works during his time.

Description of Raags in Man Kautuhal

According to Man Kautuhal there are six main Raags which are considered to be Shuddha Ragas : (1) Bhairav, Sampurna Jati, (2) Malauns, Sampurna Jati, (3) Hindol, Avdav Jati, (4) Deepak, Sampurna Jati, (5) Shree, Sampurna Jati, (6) Megh, Avdav Jati.

Each of these Ragas has been discussed in considerable

1. Faqueerullah : Raag Darpan; p. 49.

depth and detail. According to another classification, Raags are classified into three parts : 1. Shuddha Raag, 2. Salang Raag, 3. Sankeerna Raag.

Suddha Raags are the six main Raags—Bhairav, Malkauns, Hindol, Deepak, Shree, Megh,

Salang are the Raginis and Putras of Shuddha Raags. Whatever has been composed after these Ragas is considered to be Sankeerna Raag. A Raag which is composed through the initiative of a musician who combines several Raags is called Sankeerna.

The Raags are further sub-divided into three categories : (1) Sampurna (2) Shadav (3) Avdav

Each Raga has five Raginis and eight Putras except Shree Raag which has nine Putras.

Raginis of Bhairav Raag

Bhairav Raag has been described as a basic Raag. According to another opinion, Shree Raag is the main Raag. Following are the Raginis of Bhairav Raag :

(1) Bengali (2) Bhairvi (3) Bilavali (4) Dristikar or Deshkar (5) Berari (6) Saindhvi.

Putras-8

(1) Madh (2) Devsakh (3) Lalit (4) Madhav (5) Bilawal (6) Harsh (7) Pancham (8) Tilak.

Raginis of Raag Malkauns-5

(1) Gaudkri (2) Gandhari (3) Gauri (4) Andhiyali (5) Dhanasri.

Putras-8

(1) Maru (2) Madhmad (3) Prabal (4) Mishtang (5) Chandrakosh (6) Bhor (7) Nandan (8) Khokhar.

Raginis of Hindol Raag-5

(1) Tilangi (2) Devgiri (3) Basanti (4) Sinduri (5) Abheri.

Putras-8

(1) Mangal (2) Chandrabhan (3) Sobhang (4) Anand (5) Vibhas (6) Gaura (7) Pradhan (8) Vinod.

Raginis of Raag Deepak-5

(1) Kamodni (2) Patmanjari (3) Todi (4) Gurjari (5) Kaveli or Kabeli.

Putras-8

(1) Kanwal (2) Kumbher (3) Sam (4) Kuntal (5) Kilank (6) Lahal (7) Champak (8) Himal.

Raginis of Raag Shree-6

(1) Berari (This Ragini has been described as a Ragini of Raag Bhairav also) (2) Karnati (3) Sabheri (4) Gauri (5) Ramkri or Ramkali (6) Sinduri.

Putras-9

(1) Sindhu (2) Malu (3) Gaund (4) Gambhir (5) Gunsakhi (6) Vikat (7) Kalyan (8) Kumbh (9) Agat.

Raginis of Raag Megh-5

(1) Malhar (2) Sorthi (3) Asawari (4) Gayak (5) Mukutmali

Putras-8

(1) Nistar (2) Kanhra (3) Sarang (4) Kedara (5) Gaud Malhar (6) Jalandhur (7) Shankarabharana (8) Shahana.

The author of Raag Darpan states that several varieties and variations of each Raag are described in Man Kautuhal. These Raags are composed by combining that particular Raag with the other Raags. Hundreds of such Raags have been described in the book. Following are two examples :

I. Five varieties of Kanhra according to Man Kautuhal :

1. Shuddha Kanhra—It is not combined with any other Raag.

(2) Adana—A combination of Kanhra and Malhar.

3. Bageshri—A combination of Shuddha Kanhra and Dhanasri.

4. Shahana—A combination of Kanhra and Farodast.

5. Puriya—A combination of Kanhra, Dhaulshri and Mangal Ishtak.

II. Five varieties of Kamod according to Man Kautuhal :

1. Kamod—A combination of Gaur and Bilawal.

2. Shuddha Kamod—A combination of Shuddha and Kamod.

3. Kalyan Vinod Kamod—A combination of Kalyan and Kamod.

4. Sawant Kamod—A combination of Sawant and Kamod.

5. Tilak Kamod—A combination of Kamod and Khat Raag.

Faqueerullah further states that in Man Kautuhal countless Salang and Sankeerna Raags have been described which were popular when this work was compiled. He has attempted to translate the details of these Raags. For example :

Malshree—A combination of Saraswati, Kedara and Shankarabharana.

Dhanashri—A combination of Gauri, Maulshri and Jaitshree.

Jaitshree—A combination of Dhol, Berari and Deshkar.

Dholshri—A combination of Berari and Jaitshri.

After the description of different Sankeerna Raags, Faqueerullah has described the Raags which were innovated by some other famous musicians.

Nayak Bakshoo has innovated three Raags :

(1) Bahaduri—This Raag was composed by combining Todi with Deshkar, and it was named after Sultan Bahadur Gujrati.

(2) Kanhra—It was a combination of Shyam and Kumbhavati.

(3) Kalyan—Regarding this Raag the author states that he does not have much information about it.

Tansen composed Raag Darbari Kanhra which, according to the author, was a combination of Malhar, Kalyan, Asawari and Devgandhar.

Sheikh Bahauddeen Zakaria had composed Maltani Dhanashri by combining Dhanashri with Malshri.

Raags Innovated by Faqueerullah

Faqueerullah writes that he had also tried to compose few Raags by combining different Raags. Four such Raags are mentioned, which are given below :

(1) Jait Basant—A combination of Jaitshri, Hindol and Kedara.

(2) Saindhvi—A combination of Jaitshri, Kalyan, Puriya Dhanashri and Basant.

(3) Sundravati—A combination of Gaud Sarang, Bhakhra, Suhu, Bilawal and Devgiri.

(4) Adana Kedara—A combination of Raags Adana and Kedara.

The third chapter of Raag Darpan deals with the description of different seasons which are asociated with various Raags, the description of Grams, and inauspicious words which have been prohibited in different styles of singing. According to the author the scholars of earlier times have divided the year into six seasons.' For each season they have determined a Raag, Raginis and their Putras. For each Gram also a season has been specified. Faqueerullah is of the opinion that these rules were framed by some of the ancient scholars and medieval Nayaks, like Baiju and Gopal.

Six Seasons and their Raags

Season	Month	Raag
1. Basant Ritu	Chaitra-Vaisakh	Raag Hindol, its Raginis and Putras.
2. Greeshma Ritu	Jaisth-Asarh	Raag Deepak, its Raginis and Putras.
3. Pawas Ritu	Sawan-Bhadon	Raag Megh, its Raginis and Putras.
4. Sheet Ritu	Kuar-Kartik	Raag Shree, its Raginis and Putras.
5. Hemant Ritu	Aghan-Poos	Raag Malkauns, its Raginis and Putras.
6. Shishir Ritu	Magh-Falgun	Raag Bhairav, its Raginis and Putras.

Grams and their Seasons

	Gram	*Season*	*Time*
1.	Shadaj Gram	Hemant Ritu	Morning
2.	Madhyam Gram	Greeshma Ritu	Noon
3.	Gandhar Gram	Pawas Ritu	Evening

In the fourth chapter the description of Svara and different forms of singing is given. The term Svara has been defined as below :

Svara—There are seven notes or svaras in Indian music and they have been assigned distinct names.

Each svara has been produced from various parts of the human body, such as stomach, navel, throat and forehead. Besides it is also thought that they have been taken from animal voices. The details of each svara are given below :

Shadaj—It has been established on the fourth shruti. The sound of this svara originates from the navel, goes to the throat, to the chest, to the palate, and then comes out of the mouth through the tongue. It resembles the voice of peacock.

Rishabh—Three shrutis have been assigned for Rishabh. The sound of this svara starts from the navel and goes through the throat and head before it comes out of the mouth. It is believed to resemble the cuckoo's sound.

Gandhar—There are two shrutis for Gandhar. The sound of this svara starts at the navel, goes to the throat, from there to the forehead and comes out of the mouth. It has been taken from the sound of goat.

Madhyam—It contains four shrutis. To produce this svara the sound starts from the navel and stays in the chest, where it becomes Madhyam.

Pancham—Pancham also has four shrutis. The sound originating from the navel, goes into the flanks, from there to the head, returns from the head to the chest, where it stays and becomes Pancham.

Dhaivat—Three shrutis are alloted to the svara. To produce this svara the sound travels from the nose to throat and head, then it passes in the chest. This svara resembles the sound produced by horse.

Nishad—For Nishad two shrutis have been alloted. To produce this svara the sound is initiated from the nose, from where it goes to the throat and palate and then reaches the head where it becomes Nishad.

Three forms of abovementioned svaras have been discussed : (1) Shuddha (2) Komal (3) Tivra.

Forms and Styles of Singing

While describing the Margi and Desi sangeet the author has said that the practice and study of Margi sangeet was virtually stopped during his time. But it was still marginally traceable in some parts of Deccan. In those parts of Deccan the Margi sangeet was practised and publicized from the beginning to a much greater extent as compared to north India. However, the author states that during his time Desi music had begum to gain considerable popularity.

Following are the forms described by Faqueerullah :[1]

(1) Suraj Prakash (2) Chandra Prakash (3) Shruti Bhadra (4) Raag Kudam or Gram (5) Jhoomra (6) Swar Adrutni (7) Prabandh (8) Man (9) Dhruvapad (10) Chhand (11) Dhruva (12) Chutkala (13) Sadhar Chutkala (14) Qaul (15) Tarana (16) Khyal (17) Naqsh (18) Qalbana (19) Nigar (20) Tillana (21) Sohela (22) Baseet (23) Vishnu Pad (24) Trivat (25) Kane (26) Lachari (27) Gujri (28) Katarkha (29) Sadra (30) Bal-Leela (31) Tappa (32) Mankal (33) Bar (34) Zakri.[2]

The author has said that there were several more forms of singing described in Man Kautuhal and other Granthas, but he copied only these styles which were popular during his time.

In the fifth chapter, description of musical instruments, Nayaks and Nayikas is given. The author has classified musical instruments into four categories. He has described the characteristics of these groups and instruments in considerable detail. He has further listed the musical instruments in details, which were popular during his time. Following is the author's narration of those instruments.

Jantar—It consisted of a hollowed piece of wood about a yard in length, having one dried pumpkin fixed on each end. Sixteen wooden pieces are fixed on the main stick of the intrument which is called Sar. Five iron strings are also clamped on the stick. Manipulation of the wooden pieces produces higher and lower musical notes.

Been—It is like Jantar, but it has only three strings.

Kinar Been—In this instrument there is one hollowed piece of wood, three dried pumpkins and two strings.

1. Faqueeruliah : Raag Darpan; pp. 38-52.
2. More details of these forms are given in Section II of this study.

Sur Been—It is just like Been except that it does not have the wooden pieces.

Abvritti—Its wooden piece is shorter than surbeen.

Rebab—It consisted of six gut strings. A couplet has also been composed in praise of Rebab.

Sur Mandal—Its structure is similar to Qanoon except that it has one additional string. Some people used iron strings while others used Brass or Gut strings also in this instrument.

Sarang—It is shorter than Rebab.

Pinak—It is made of a long stick.

Dhevti—It has two dried pumpkins and two strings.

Kangura—It is like Been but has two gut strings.

Tambura—It has five iron or copper strings.

Pakhawaj—It is the first vitat instrument. It is believed that it was made by Mahadev and it is used for providing Tal to all types of dancing.

Awaz—It resembles Tabla and is made of hollow wood.

Dhol, Daf and Dholki—Dholki is smaller dhol.

Ardhawaz—It is half of Awaz.

Khanjari—It is a small Daf and has Jhanjh (cymbals) attached to it.

Tal—It is made of copper and has the shape of a bowl, having a wide mouth.

Kath Tal—It has four fish shaped wooden pieces, in which fcur pieces of stone are studded.

Jal-Tarang—These are the cups made of china clay.

Shahna—It looks like flute and is played by mouth.

In the second part of this chapter the author has described the different varieties of Nayaks and Nayikas along with their qualities and defects. It is an interesting and elaborate portion of the chapter. It might be useful fo the scholars of Hindi literature.

The sixth chapter is about the defects and qualities of musicians which is almost similar to the description as given in Tohfat-ul-Hind which is going to be discussed in the second chapter of this study.

The seventh chapter deals with the different types of voices of musicians. The author has categorised the voices of musicians into four types : (1) Kahahal (Khahul, according to Sangeet Ratnakar). (2) Narat (3) Yavnek (Bombuk according to Sangeet Ratnakar) (4) Mishrak.

Kahahal is of three varieties : (1) Madhur (2) Sukmarya (3) Aral (Adilya according to Sangeet Ratnakar).

Narat is also divided into four types : (1) Tristhan (2) Ghana (3) Gambhir (4) Leen.

In the eighth chapter, the author has given the description of different classifications of musicians. The musicians, according to the qualities of voice, are divided into fifteen categories :

(1) Mrichshit (Mrisht according to Sangeet Ratnakar) (2) Madhur (3) Jhampal (Chehtal, accordjng to Sangeet Ratnakar) (4) Tristhan (5) Sukhavah (6) Barjar (Prachur) (7) Komal (8) Gaadh (not clear) (9) Shravuk (10) Karuna (11) Lahan (Ghan) (12) Sugandh (Snigdh, according to Sangeet Ratnakar) (13) Sulakshana (14) Rikt-Jagat (Rakti-Yukt, according to Sangeet Ratnakar) (15) Asthiman (Chhaviman, according to Sangeet Ratnakar).

The musicians are classified in different ways. According to one classification the musicians are of two types : (1) Gunkar (2) Gandharva.

According to another classification, the musicians can be divided into three categories : (1) Uttam (2) Madhyam (3) Adham.

While in another classification the musicians are classified in five categories : (1) Shikshakar (2) Anukar (3) Rasik (4) Ranjak (5) Bhavuk.

Three types of Gayaks are described : (1) Ekal (2) Jamal or Yamal (3) Vrind.

Definition of Vrind

Faqueerullah states that according to Shastras when a group of vocalists and instrumentalists assemble and perform together, it is called Vrind. Vrind is of three kinds—(1) Uttam (2) Madhyam (3) Nikrisht.

In the ninth chapter the author has given a detailed description of Vrind, and he states that in earlier periods the rules of Vrind performances were followed correctly. In those days the vocalists used to sit in the front and instrumentalists on the back side. But in the author's time musicians were not following these rules. They were performing without the proper knowledge of shastras. Consequently, the author felt that there was little to be expected in the form of coaching from such people. In addition to this, the author has given a detailed description for the composition of Vrind.

In the tenth chapter of Raag Darpan the author has given the description of the musicians before and during the author's time. He has given an account of some of the musicians who were not alive at that time. He has further given an account of those musicians who were living and performing during his time. These descriptions are fairly elaborate and informative.

In the end of the concluding chapter, the author has given a short description of Persian music. In this part some of the forms of Persian music have been discussed. He has compared Persian Maqams with their parallel Indian Raags.

The foregoing study and analysis of Raag Darpan leads us to the following insights and conclusions :

(1) During the author's time the Raag Ragini system for classifying Raags was very much in vogue, whereas the Thaat system was not utilized. The names of different Raags and Raginis are almost the same as given in Tohfat-ul-Hind. However the description of these names in Tohfat-ul-Hind are more clear and detailed.

(2) Dhruvapad was considered to be a musical form of a very high order and was very popular during the author's time. While discussing this style the author states: "Dhruvapad has been so much practised as a form of music by the elite and the common musician that all other forms of music have been relegated into background"[1].

(3) The other forms and styles of music which have been mentioned in Raag Darpan are known and popular even today, except a few of them. For such few forgotten styles also some musicians who were familiar which them could be found until a few years ago.

(4) A very singnificant point which comes to light and

1. Faqueerullah: Raag Darpan; p. 39

contradicts the popular and widely believed notion about Aurangzeb's hostility to music and musicians is that the various statements by Faqueerullah reveal Aurangzeb's fondness for music and musicians, and the frequent visits of musicians to his court. For example, while describing Khushhal Khan Faqueerullah says : "Khushhal Khan is the most outstanding and unparalleled musician, and he has a very good rapport with the Emperor". At another place, while concluding the description of musicians, he says : "There are probably many more musicians in the country, but I have no information about them, since they have not visited the Emperor's court".

(5) The author has described all categories of known instruments of his time, but he has made no mention of Sitar and Tabla. An instrument similar to Tabla has been described as Awaz. The absence of the description of Sitar could lead to the conclusion that either Sitar was not popular at that time or was invented later.

(6) A study of Raag Darpan makes it abundantly clear that it is not merely an excellent source of information about music of its time, but also incorporates in considerable detail all the main points of Man Kautuhal which was written in between 1486 to 1518 A.D. Thus it may be said that Raag Darpan is an authentic source for the historical development of Hindustani music during the sixteenth, seventeenth and eighteenth centuries. It can, therefore, be considered as a comprehensive and complete work which is of great relevance to the researchers and musicologists.

CHAPTER II

Tohfat-ul-Hind

VARIOUS manuscripts of Tohfat-ul-Hind are available in different libraries, but there is difference of opinion about its author. In one manuscript the author's name is Mirza Jaan, and according to another manuscript the author is Mirza Khan. In the Berlin manuscript the author's name is Mirza Mohammad. The name of the author given in Riew's catalogue is Mirza Khan.[1]

The author of Tohfat-ul-Hind has stated that this book was written during Aurangzeb's period, but the correct date of its writing is not mentioned. According to another opinion, during Akbar's time, one of the grandsons of Abdur-Rahim Khan-e-Khanan was named Mirza Khan, who was alive in 1055 A.H. (1645-46 A.D.). But it cannot be said with certainty that he was the same person who wrote this book. In one of the manuscripts it has been stated that this was written for Aurangzeb's third son Mohammad Azam, while in another manuscript there is mention of Moizuddin Jahandarshah.[2]

One portion of Tohfat-ul-Hind, which deals with Hindi grammar, was edited and published from Shanti Niketan. Syed Masood Hasan Rizvi has translated its grammar portion in Urdu. However, the best and most comprehensive work on this manuscript has been done by Dr. Nurul Hasan Ansari. He has edited and published the book from Iran.

According to Syed Masood Hasan Rizvi, Tohfat-ul-Hind was written for Aurangzeb, but in the opinion of Ansari, it

1. Ansari, N.H. : Tohfat-ul-Hind, Preface.
2. Ibid, Preface.

must have been written for Mohammad Azam, Aurangzeb's third son, because he was a great admirer of Indian literature, poetry and music.

In addition to the points mentioned above, further evidence which supports the possibility of the book being written for Azam Shah is that another manuscript on the art of music was written by Mulla Aiwaz Beg which was dedicated to Mohammad Azam. This manuscript is available in the library of Dargah of Ucha Sharif (an old town near Bahawalpur). There are 13 chapters and a preface in this manuscript.[1]

As mentioned earlier, Mohammad Azam was very fond of Indian literature and an Indian poet by the name of Nawaz was one of his courtiers. In accordance with the wishes of the prince, he translated Shakuntala from Sanskrit to Persian. He also edited the Sat-Sai of Behari and gave it the title "Sat-Sai Azam Shahi".[2]

The writer of Tohfat-ul-Hind has not given reference of other books in any of the chapters, except in the chapter on music, in which he has referred to four classic books on music, namely, Sangeet Darpan, Man Kautuhal, Sabha Vinod, Ragarnav and Raag Darpan.

Tohfat-ul-Hind contains seven parts : 1. Ilm-e-Pingle, 2. Ilm-e-Tuk 3. Ilm-e-Alankar 4. Sringar Ras 5. Ilm-e-Sangeet 6. Ilm-e-Kok 7. Samudrik Shastra.

The first four parts of the book have been devoted to a detailed description of Hindi language, its grammar, alphabetical orders, aesthetics, etc. The fifth part of the book is on the subject of music. This part is based on the ten detailed chapters on different aspects of the art of Mousiqui (music).

Sapt Adhyay

According to the author there are seven Usools (rules) and Arkans (fundamentals) of the art of music, and so this part of the book has been written as Sapt Adhyay. Following are the seven parts of Sapt Adhaay: (1) Swar Adhyay (2) Raag Adhyay (3) Tal Adhyay (4) Nritya Adhyay (5) Arth Adhyay (6) Bhav Adhyay (7) Isht Adhyay.

The first three parts are discussed in great detail. An

1. Ansari, N.H. : Farsi Adab Ba Ahde-Aurangzeb; p, 60.
2. Ansari, N.H, : Tohfat-ul-Hind, Praface; pp. 17-18.

abbreviated version of these three parts is given below.

Swar Adhyay

The subject of Svara and Shruti has been described very comprehensively. In the beginning of this chapter the names of seven notes are discussed, and from the seven notes three notes are selected as the basic notes : (1) The lowest note, (2) The highest note, (3) The middle note.

Above three notes have been described as Gram. Grams are of three types : (1) Shadaj Gram (2) Gandhar Gram (3) Madhyam Gram.

There are three Sthanas of these Grams : (1) Mandra (2) Madhya (3) Tar.

Every note has been derived from particular sounds produced by animals and brids. Shadaja Svara has been derived from the sound of peacock, Rishabh from the sound of cuckoo, Gandhar from the sound of goat. Madhyam from the sound of falcon, pancham from the sound of koel, Dhaiwat from the sound of horse, and Nishad from the sound of elephant.

Shruti

This is an elaborate protion of the chapter in which the names of 22 Shrutees are given. The names of Shrutees of each Svara are as follows :

(1) Shadaj	— 4 shrutees	— Tivra, Kummudni, Mandra, Chhandovati
(2) Rishabh	— 3 shrutees	— Dayavati, Ranjani, Raktika
(3) Gandhar	— 2 shrutees	— Raudri, Krodha
(4) Madhyam	— 4 shrutees	— Vajra, Prasarini, Preeti, Marjani
(5) Pancham	— 4 shrutees	— Kshiti, Raktika, Sandeepni Alapni
(6) Dhaiwat	— 3 shrutees	— Madanti, Rohini, Ramya
(7) Nishad	— 2 shrutees	— Ugra, Kshobhini

Murchhna

The definition of Murchhna is not very clear. The author states that the intervals between two Svaras is called Murchhna. Example—If we sing Shadaj and then Rishabh, we stay for some moments in between these two notes. This interval has been defined as Murchhna. Similarly the singing of notes one by one in order has been described as Murchhna. There are seven murchhnas of each Gram.

Raag Adhyay

This chapter is very comprehensive, and is one of the most well written chapters of the book. A study of this chapter brings out a clear picture of the classification of Raag and Ragini system during the medieval times. Following three Jatis of Raags have heen described : (1) Avdav (2) Shadav (3) Sampurna.

Classification of Raags

Raags are classified in three categories : (1) Shuddha (2) Salang (3) Sankeerna.

Shuddha Raags

The Raags which cannot be combined with other Raags are called Shuddha Raags. Shuddha Raags are divided into two parts : (1) Shuddha (2) Maha Shuddha.

Shuddha—These Raags are not mixed with other Raags but their notes can be vikrit. Example—Raag Todi. Maha Shuddha—These are the Raags which are not combined with other Raags and at the same time all their Svaras are also Shuddha. Example—Kanhra and Sarang.

Salang Raags

The Raags which have the shadow or colour of other Raags. Example—Shree Raag, which has the colour of Raag Gauri.

Sankeerna Raags

The Raags which are constructed by combining other Raags and Raginis are called Sankeerna Raags. Sankeerna Raags are of two types—(1) Sankeerna (2) Maha Sankeerna. Sankeerna—The Raags which are constructed by combining only Shuddha Raags are called Sankeerna Raags. Example—Raag Bhairav which is the combination of Todi and Kanhra (these two Raags are Shuddha Raags).

Maha Sankeerna—These are the Raags which are composed by combining and mixing Shuddha with Salang with Sankeerna or two Salang with Sankeerna or combining two Snakeerna Raags.

The Classification of Musicians

Musicians are classified in five catagories : (1) Swechha

chari[1] (2) Ankar[2] (3) Rasik (4) Ranjak (5) Bhavuk.

According to another classification the musicians are of three types : (1) Ikal (2) Jamal (3) Vrind.

The Characteristics of Musicians

The characteristics of musicians (vocalists) are divided into two categories : (1) The characteristics based on the quality of voice. (2) The characteristics based on competence.

In the first category there are 14 types of musicians. (1) Mrisht (2) Madhur (3) Jhampal (Chehal of Sangeet Ratnaker) (4) Tristhan (5) Sukhavah (6) Komal (7) Shravuk (8) Karuna (9) Ghat or Ghad (10) Snigdh (11) Gaarh (12) Sulakshana or Slakshana (13) Prajar or Prachur (14) Rakhi-Yukt. In the second category 16 varieties of musicians are described.

Defects of Musicians

The defects of the musicians are also classified in two categories.

(1) The defects of musicians based on deficiencies in voice.

(2) The defects based on incompetence of musicians.

In the first category there are seven types of musicians, such as, Rochhit, A-Sthir, Nis-sar, Kagi, Karsh, etc.

In the second category following twenty five types of musicians are described :

(1) Sandisht (2) Uddhrisht (3) Bheet (4) Shankit (5) Kampit (6) Karali (7) Kagi (8) Kapil (9) Betal (10) Karabh (11) Uddanda (12) Jhombak (13) Vakri (14) Prasari (15) Nimilak (16) Apswar (17) Veras (18) Avyavasthit (19) Avyakt (20) Sthan bhrasht (21) Anavdhan (22) Sutkari or Siptkari (23) Mishrak (24) Sannunasik (25) Karkash.

Vrind Sangeet

An ensemble of of musicians (vocalists and instrumentalists) is called Vrind. There are three types of Vrind.

(1) **Uttam Vrind**—This consists of four highly accomplished male vocalists, eight vocalists of medium standards, twelve female vocalists, whose voices are sweet and soft, four flute players and four Mridang players.

(2) **Madhyam Vrind**—This has half the numbers of the

1. This term has been described in Sangeet Ratnakar as Shikshakar.
2. This term has been described in Sangeet Ratnakar as Anukar.

Uttama Vrind.

(3) **Adham Vrind**—This has half the numbers of Madhyama Vrind.

Vrind of Women

These are of three types :

(1) **Uttam**—It has two accomplished female vocalists, four vocalists of medium standards, two flute players and two Mridang players.

(2) **Madhyam**—It has only one accomplished female vocalist and the remaining composition is the same as in Uttam Vrind.

(3) **Adham or Nikrisht**—This has a lesser number of performers compared to the above two Vrinds.

If a Vrind has a large number of performers than the Uttam Vrind, it is called Kolahal (noise and tumult). The chapter on Vrind is very detailed and clear. It gives highly useful and relevant information.

After Vrind, there is description of Vakgeykara (composer) and the qualities of an ideal Vakgeykara have been given in detail. This part is identical with the description of Vakgeykara in Sangeet Ratnakar of Pandit Sarangdev.

Forms and Styles of Singing

The author has divided the forms and styles of singing into two parts :

(1) Those styles and forms which were popular and practical during ancient and medieval periods. These styles were in the Prakrit language. They are of seven types : (1) Geet (2) Jhoomra (3) Chhand (4) Dhruva (5) Matha (6) Dhva (7) Prabandh.

(2) Those forms which were popular during the author's own period—(1) Dhruvapad (2) Trivat (3) Phoolbandh (4) Jugalbandh (5) Vishnupad (6) Khyal (7) Qaul (8) Tarana (9) Jakrior Zakri (10) Kadhka (11) Bagad (12) Baad or Bar.

Names of Gods and Goddesses of Music who are Considered Creators of Music

(1) Someshvar (2) Bharat (3) Hanuman (4) Parvati (5) Sarasvati (6) Durga (7) Vayu (8) Shesh (9) Narad (10) Kallinatha (11) Tumburu (12) Kashyap (13) Shardul (14) Kohal

(15) Atotra (16) Ha-Ha (17) Hu-Hu (18) Ravana (19) Disha (20) Arjun.

Categories of Musicians of Medieval Period

(1) Gandharva (2) Gunkar (3) Kalawant (4) Kawwal (5) Dadhi or Dharhi (6) Pandit.

Names of Famous Nayaks

(1) Gopal (2) Ameer Khusrau (3) Baiju (4) Bhannu (5) Pandvi (6) Bakshoo (7) Lohang (8) Charju (2) Bhagwan (10) Dhondhi (11) Dhalu.

Names of Musicians of the Period of Jalaluddeen Akbar

(1) Tansen (2) Subhan Khan (3) Swargban Khan Fatahpuri (4) Chand Khan (5) Suraj Khan (6) Tan Tarang Khan (7) Madan Rai (8) Ramdas Bheediya (9) Baz Bahadur (10) Mian Chandu (11) Mian Daood (12) Mulla Ishaq (13) Sheikh Khizr (14) Sheikh Bhanju (15) Hasan Khan Patni (16) Surat Sen (17) Lala and Devi (18) Mirza Aquil.

Raags, Raginis, Putras, and Bharyas

This is an elaborate chapter in which the Raags are classified according to different Mats (opinions). A study of this chapter reveals that at the time when Tohfat-ul-Hind was written, the system of Raags and Raginis was very much in vogue. The musicians had thorough familiarity with this system and they followed its rules in their performances. This subject has been given a very intensive coverage in the book.

In the introduction of this chapter, the author has given the genesis and definition of the term Raag. In his opinion Raag is the name of a Persian Muqam and in Hindustani music there are six main Raags. Each Raag has five Raginis and eight Putras.

According to other opinions there are six Raags, six Raginis and eight Putras. Each Putra has one Bharya. Every Raag is practised in a particular season. Each of the Raags has also been picturized in a fanciful imagination in Ragmala, which have also been described by the author.

There are four Mats regarding Raag Ragini System : (1) Kallinath Mat (2) Someshvara Mat (3) Hanuman Mat (4) Bharat Mat.

Whereas the author has described each of the Raags, he has given the most detailed account of the Hanuman Mat. During the author's time the Hanuman Mat was most frequently followed by the musicians.

Details of Raags According to Hanuman Mat

According to Hanuman Mat there are six Raags in Hindustani Music—(1) Bhairav (2) Malkauns (3) Hindol (4) Deepak (5) Shree (6) Megh.

Following are the main features of the above mentioned Raags.

Raag Bhairav—Mahadeva or Lord Shiva is considered to be the creator of this Raag;[1] Svaras—Dha Ni Sa Ga Ma; Grah Svar—Dhaivat; Season for singing—Sharad Ritu; Picture in Ragmala—A handsome male who resembles Lord Shiva, looks like a saint. There are bangles on his wrists, wearing Janev (the sacred thread) and has Tilak on his forehead. A snake is wrapped round his neck. A skin of elephant is wrapped on his body, or he is using the skin as carpet, and sitting on it. He is wearing a necklace of heads of human beings, and the river Ganga is coming out of his Jatas (hair on the head).

Raag Malkauns—This Raag has come out of the mouth of Mahadeva, Hari or Kanha (Krishna); Svaras—Sa Re Ga Ma Pa Dha Ni; Grah Svar—Shadaj; Jati—Sampurna; Season of singing—Shishir Ritu; Picture in Ragmala—A healthy and strong male wearing blue dress, has frightening expressions, as he is intoxicated with liqour. He has a stick in his hand, and has the heads of his enemies in a garland around his neck along with pearls of Marwarid.

Raag Hindol—This Raag is believed to have originated from the body of Lord Bramha. According to another belief, it has emanated from Bramha's navel; Svaras—Sa Ga Ma Pa Ni; Grah Svar—Shadaj; Jati—Avdav; Season of singing—the first part of the day in Basant Ritu; Picture in Ragmala—A young handsome male wearing yellow dress is sitting on the swing and

1. It may be noted here that Bhairav Raag has been described as Avdav Raag, consisting of five notes, whereas Malkauns has been descibed as Sampurna Raag consisting of seven notes. The author of Usulun-Naghmat-e-Asifi has also discussed this point, which has been elaborated in the next chapter.

some beautiful women are singing and playing instruments, and are rocking his swing.

Raag Deepak—This Raag has come out of the eyes of the sun; Svaras—Sa Re Ga Ma Pa Dha Ni; Grah Svar—Shadaj; Jati—Sampurna; Season of singing—noon hour during the summer; Picture in Ragmala—A male of reddish complexion, wearing colourful dresses and necklace of pearls, who is riding an elephant. He is accompanied by several women.

Raag Shree—This Raag is born out of the Prithvi (earth); Svaras—Sa Re Ga Ma Pa Dha Ni; Grah Svar—Shadaj; Jati—Sampurna; Season of singing—the last part of the day of Him Ritu; Picture in Ragmala—a handsome male wearing a necklace of fine polished beads. He is seated on throne, is dressed in red, and is surrounded by many men who are singing.

Raag Megh—This Raag has emerged from the head of Bramha; Svaras—Dha Ni Sa Re Ga; Grah Svar—Dhaivat; Jati—Avdav; Season of singing—Varsha Ritu; Picture in Ragmala—A handsome man who has his hair tied up like a beautiful turban, and he has an unsheathed sword in his hand.

Raginis of Hanuman Mat

According to Hanuman Mat each Raag has five Raginis. These Raginis are also described in detail. Following is their description :

Raginis of Raag Bhairav

(1) **Bhairvi** : Jati—Sampurna; Svaras—Ma Pa Dha Ni Sa Re Ga; Grah—Madhyam; Season of singing—Sheet Ritu, morning time; Picture in Ragmala—a young and beautiful maid of yellowish complexion, who has long hair. She is wearing red blouse and white sari. Her head is adorned with a garland of champa flowers. She is seated on the peak of a mountain and is worshipping the Linga of Mahadev. Nearby some people are singing and playing Manjeera.

(2) **Barari**—The Sanskrit name for Raag Barari is Barati; Jati—Sampurna; Svaras—Sa Re Ga Ma Pa Dha Ni; Grah—Shadaj; Season of singing—evenings of Sheet Ritu, Picture in Ragmala—a beautiful woman, wearing bangles and necklace of flowers of Kalpvriksha.[1] Her dress is white and she is sit-

1. A mythological tree or plant is supposed to grant all desires.

ting with her Nayak (companion).

(3) **Madhmad** : Jati—Sampurna; Svaras—Ma Pa Dha Ni Sa Re Ga; Grah—Madhyam; Season of singing—morning of Sheet Ritu; Picture in Ragmala—a beautiful maid with attractive eyes, wearing a yellow dress. She has a saffron Tilak on her forehead, and also has saffron on her body, relaxed and enjoying the company of the Nayak.

(4) **Saindhvi** : Jati—Sampurna ; Svaras—Sa Re Ga Ma Pa Dha Ni ; Grah—Shadaj; Time—in the last part of the day of Sheet Ritu; Picture in Ragmala—A beautiful woman, wearing red sari, is stitting and waiting for her Nayak. She has a garland in her hand and is absorbed in the thoughts of Mahadev.

(5) **Bangal** : Jati—Sampurna; Svaras—Sa Re Ga Ma Pa Dha Ni; Grah—Shadaj; Season of singing—last part of the day in Sheet Ritu. Picture in Ragmala—A beautiful woman, who has applied ashes on her face like yogis. She has tied up her hair over her head as a bun. She has Trishul in her left hand and a lotus in her right hand. She is wearing a saffron colour dress.

Raginis of Raag Malkauns

(1) **Todi** : Jati—Sampurna; Svaras—Sa Re Ga Ma Pa Dha Ni; Grah—Shadaj; Season of singing—second part of the day in Sheet Ritu; Picture in Ragmala—a beautiful and slender woman wearing white sari and blouse made of animal skin. She has applied ashes of camphor on her body. She is playing Been in a lonely forest and deer enchanted by her music are sitting in front of her.

(2) **Gauri** : Jati—Avdav; Svaras—Sa Ga Ma Dha Ni; Grah—Shadaj; Season of singing—last part of the day of winter. Picture in Ragmala—a young maiden, having a tender body and greenish complexion, dressed in white and wearing earrings of the mango blossom, she wishes to sing but because of intoxication she is unable to sing.

(3) **Gunkri or Gunkali** : It is often called Kungli; Jati—Avdav; Svaras—Ni Sa Ga Ma Pa; Grah—Nishad; Season of singing—mornings of Shishir Ritu; Picture in Ragmala—a

woman, who is separated from her companion and is weeping. Due to her sorrow she has become very frail and weak.

(4) **Khambhavati** : Jati—Shadav; Svaras—Dha Ni Sa Re Ga Ma; Grah—Dhaivat; Season of singing—Shishir Ritu (after midnight); Picture in Ragmala—a beautiful woman who is leading a luxurious life and is always absorbed in singing and dancing. Sha wears a green blouse, white sari and beautiful garments and has a Bindi on her forehead.

(5) **Kukubh** : Jati—Sampurna; Svaras—Dha Ni Sa Re Ga Ma Pa; Grah—Dhaivat; Season of singing—last part of the night in Shishir Ritu; Picture in Ragmala—a beautiful healthy woman with attractive eyes, is comfortably seated by the side of her Nayak.

Raginis of Raag Hindol

(1) **Ramkri** : It is often called Ramkali; Jati—Avdav; Svaras—Sa Ga Ma Dha Ni; Grah—Shadaj; Season of singing —morning of Basant Ritu; Picture in Ragmala—a beautiful maiden of yellowish complexion, is wearing blue dress. She has a musk Tilak on her forehead. She had been waiting for her companion, who has now arrived and has his forehead on her feet, but she is still angry and is not looking at him.

(2) **Des or Desh** : Jati—Avdav: Svaras—Ga Ma Pa Dha Ni Sa; Grah—Gandhar; Season of singing—beginning of the day of Basant Ritu; Picture in Ragmala—a strong, good looking angry woman with an unsheathed sword. She always applies clay to her body and arms. She always dominates her Nayak, and she can do wrestling and acrobatics.

(3) **Lalit** : Jati—Avdav; Svaras—Dha Ni Sa Ga Ma; Grah—Dhaivat; Season of singing—Basant Ritu, morning; Picture in Ragmala—A dainty woman with a silver complexioned body and slender waist. She has lovely eyes and is adorned with hundreds of items of jewellery. She is wearing a red dress and has garland of flowers round her neck.

(4) **Beravar** : Some musicians call it Beravari, but its most popular name is Bilaval or Bilavali; Jati—Sampurna; Svaras—Dha Ni Sa Re Ga Ma Pa; Grah—Dhaivat; Season of singing—morning of Basant; Picture in Ragmala—A dark complexioned slender woman, wearing colourful dress and waiting for her Nayak.

(5) **Pat Manjari** : Jati—Sampurna; Svaras—Dha Ni Sa Re Ga Ma Pa; Grah—Dhaivat; Season of singing—a woman dressed like yogis is remembering her separated Nayak. She is sitting, having a garland of flowers on her neck of which all the flowers have dried.

Raginis of Raag Deepak

(1) **Desi** : Jati—Shadav; Svaras—Re Ga Ma Dha Ni Sa; Grah—Rishabh; Season of singing—forenoon of summer. Picture in Ragmala—A beautiful woman wearing white and green dress. She is also wearing jewellery.

(2) **Kamod** : Jati—Sampurna; Svaras—Dha Ni Sa Re Ga Ma: Grah—Dhaivat; Picture in Ragmala—a healthy woman of yellowish complexion, wearing a white blouse and red sari. She is sitting in a forest all alone, waiting for her Nayak. She is frightened and is weeping.

(3) **Nat** : Jati—Sampurna; Svaras—Sa Ni Dha Pa Ma Ga Re; Grah—Shadaj; Season of singing—summer in the last part of the day; Picture in Ragmala—a pink complexioned young woman, decorated with jewellery, wearing a man's dress, riding a horse, and fighting the enemies with an unsheathed sword in the battle field.

(4) **Kedaar** : Jati—Avdav; Svaras—Ni Sa Ga Ma Pa; Grah—Nishad; Season of singing—midnight of Greeshma Ritu; Picture in Ragmala—a yogi woman, whose hair are tied over her head, on which a serpent is wrapped. She is wearing a saffron robe and has a crescent shaped Tilak on her forehead. She is meditating on Mahadev with closed eyes.

(5) **Kanhra** : The Sanskrit name of this Ragini is Karnati; Jati—Sampurna; Svaras—Ni Sa Re Ga Ma Pa Dha; Grah—Nishad; Season of singing—morning hours of Greeshma Ritu. Picture in Ragmala—a man dressed in white, who has applied ashes on his body. He has an unsheathed sword in his right hand and an elephant tusk in his left hand. Sycophants are surrounding and admiring him.

Raginis of Raag Shree

(1) **Malshri** : Jati—Sampurna; Svaras—Sa Re Ga Ma Pa Dha Ni; Grah—Shadaj; Season of singing—noon hour of Him Ritu; Picture in Ragmala—a beautiful, dainty woman

of rosy complexion, wearing a yellow dress, sitting under a mango tree and laughing with her woman friends.

(2) **Marwa** : Jati—Shadav; Svaras—Sa Re Ga Ma Dha Ni; Grah—Shadaj; Season of singing—Him Ritu in the last part of the day; Picture in Ragmala—a woman wearing a golden dress, having a garland of flowers on her neck, sitting and waiting for her Nayak.

(3) **Dhanashri** : Jati—Shadav; Svaras—Sa Pa Dha Ni Re Ga; Grah—Shadaj; Season of singing—noon of Him Ritu; Picture in Ragmala—a distressed and weak woman, wearing a red dress, weeping due to sorrow of separation from her Nayak, seated under a Maulshri tree.

(4) **Basant** : Jati—Sampurna: Svaras—Sa Re Ga Ma Pa Dha Ni; Grah—Shadaj; Season of singing—forenoon of Him Ritu and Basant Ritu; Picture in Ragmala—a fair complexioned handsome man wearing red dress who has a crown of peacock feather on his head. He has a bunch of mango blossoms in his hand, and a garland of flowers on his neck. He is engrossed in enjoying himself along with singing and dancing girls in a garden. He has a folded betel leaf in left hand and is playing flute.

(5) **Asavari** : Jati—Avdav; Svaras—Dha Ni Sa Ma Pa; Grah—Dhaivat; Season of singing—forenoon of Him Ritu; Picture in Ragmala—a dark complexioned tender woman, wearing a white sari. She smears camphor ashes on her body. Long serpents are wrapped on her hands and legs.

Raginis of Raag Megh

(1) **Tunk** : Jati—Sampurna; Svaras—Sa Re Ga Ma Pa Dha Ni; Grah—Shadaj; Season of singing—a tender woman lying on a bed made of lotus flowers.

(2) **Malhar** : Jati—Avdav; Svaras—Dha Ni Re Ga Ma; Grah—Dhaivat; Season of singing—midnight of rainy season; Picture in Ragmala —a young fair complexioned woman, who has become weak and pale in the sorrow of separation with her Nayak. She is seated and is wearing the jewellery made of Jasmine flowers. She is weeping and playing Been.

(3) **Gurjari** : Jati—Sampurna; Svaras—Re Ga Ma Pa Dha Ni Sa; Grah—Rishabh; Season of singing—morning of rainy season; Picture in Ragmala—a young woman wearing yellow

blouse and red sari. Her body is adorned with jewellery.

(4) Bhopali : Jati—Sampurna; Svaras—Sa Ga Ma Dha Ni. Grah—Shadaj; Season of singing—first part of the day in rainy season; Picture in Ragmala—a beautiful woman wearing a white sari, who has applied saffron ashes to her body and has a garland of flowers round her neck. She is sitting with her arms around her Nayak's neck.

(5) **Deshkar** : Jati—Sampurna; Svaras—Sa Re Ga Ma Pa Dha Ni; Grah—Shadaj; Season of singing—the last part of night during rainy season; Picture in Ragmala—A fair beautiful woman, who has moles on her skin. She has almond eyes, silver-like body, pomegranate-like breasts, pistachio-like mouth, and is wearing a pearl necklace. She has applied sandalwood powder on her body. She is adorned with jewellery and is playing with her Nayak.

According to Hanuman Mat, these Raags and Raginis also have Putras (sons). Each Raag, Ragini has eight Putras. These are listed below :

Putras of Raag Bhirav-8

(1) Harsha (2) Tilak (3) Puriya (4) Madhav (5) Suhu (6) Balneh (7) Madh (8) Pancham.

Putras of Raag Malkauns-8

(1) Maru (2) Mewad (3) Barhans (4) Prabal (5) Chandrak (6) Nand (7) Bhanwar (8) Khokhar, or Nishtang or Vidwans.

Putras of Raag Hindol-8

(1) Chandrabimb (2) Mangal (3) Shobha (4) Anand (5) Vinod (6) Pradhan (7) Gaura (8) Vibhas or Shukra.

Putras of Raag Deepak-8

(1) Kuntal (2) Kanwal or Kamal (3) Kaling or Kalindra (4) Champak (5) Kusumbha or Kusum (6) Ram (7) Lahil (8) Himal.

Putras of Raag Shree-8

(1) Sindhu (2) Malav (3) Gaund or Kalyan or Hamir (4) Gunsagar (5) Kumbha (6) Gambhir (7) Sankar or Agad or Agat (8) Bhagra or Bigad or Vikat.

Putras of Raag Megh-8

(1) Jalandhar (2) Sarang (3) Nat Narayan (4) Shankarabharana (5) Kalyan (6) Gajdhar (7) Gandhar (8) Shahana.

Kallinatha Mat

Kallinatha has been described as a very learned saint of music. He was called Rishi Bodh. According to him there are six basic Raags and each of them has six Raginis. The six Raags identified by him are following : (1) Raag Shree (2) Raag Basant (3) Raag Pancham (4) Raag Bhairav (5) Raag Megh (6) Raag Nat-Narayan.

Three new Raags have been added to the above mentioned Raags. Three of the Raags (Shree, Bhairav and Megh) are similar to Hanuman Mat, whereas three Raags (Basant, Pancham and Nat-Narayan) are new. In Hanuman Mat, Basant has been described in Raginis, and Pancham and Nat-Narayan have been described in Putras.

According to Kallinatha Mat following are the six Raginis :

Raginis of Raag Shree-6

(1) Gauri (2) Kolahal (3) Dhol (4) Rudrani (5) Malkauns (6) Devgandhar.

Raginis of Raag Basant-6

(1) Andoli—According to some musicians it is Andhiyali. (2) Gamki (3) Patmanjari (4) Gaundkri (5) Dhamki (6) Devsakh.

Raginis of Raag Bhairav-6

(1) Bhairvi (2) Gujri (3) Bhasha (4) Bilawali (5) Karnat or Kanhra (6) Rakthansa.

Raginis of Raag Megh-6

(1) Bengali (2) Madhura (3) Kamod (4) Dhanashri (5) Devtirth (6) Devali.

Raginis of Nat-Narayan-6

(1) Tirotki (2) Tilangi or Tilgi (3) Purvi (4) Rama (5) Gandhari (6) Sindh Malleri.

The Putras of Kallinatha Mat are almost similar to the Hanuman Mat but there is a slight difference. Kalyan and Bigad have been described in place of Gaund and Shankar in Raag Shree. Devsakh, Lalit, Malkauns and Bilaval have been described in place of Tilak, Pancham, Puriya and Suhu in Raag Bhairav. Kedaar, Maru and Jal Bharat have been described in place of Nat-Narayan, Shankarabharana and Kalyan in Megh Raag. Raag Bigad of Kallinatha Mat is similar to Bhagra of Hanuman Mat, and Bilaval of Kallinatha Mat is similar to Suhu of Hanuman Mat.

There are some other similar differences, such as the Putras of Hindol have been described in Basant, Putras of Deepak have been described in Pancham, and the Putras of Malkauns have been described in Nat-Narayan. In the place of two Putras of Malkauns (Maru and Badhans), Deepak and Mushtank have been mentioned.

Someshvar Mat

The Raags of Someshvar Mat are similar to Kallinatha Mat. These are : (1) Raag Shree (2) Raag Basant (3) Raag Pancham (4) Raag Bhairav (5) Raag Megh (6) Raag Nat-Narayan.

Each of these Raags has six Raginis as the following :

Raginis of Raag Shree-6

(1) Malwi or Malwa or Marwa (2) Triveni or Trivin (3) Gauri (4) Kedaar (5) Madhumad (6) Fadka or Fadi or Fari.

Raginis of Raag Basant-6

(1) Desi (2) Devgiri (3) Bairati or Varati (4) Todka or Todi (5) Lalit (6) Hindoli or Hindol.

Raginis of Raag Bhairav-6

(1) Bhairvi (2) Gurjari or Gujari (3) Rewa (4) Gunkri or Gunkali (5) Bengali or Bengal (6) Bahuli.

Raginis of Raag Pancham-6

(1) Vibhas (2) Bhopali (3) Karnati or Kanhra (4) Barhans or Vidhwans (5) Malshri (6) Patmanjari.

Raginis of Raag Megh-6

(1) Malhar (2) Sorath (3) Saveri (4) Kaushiki or Malkauns (5) Gandhari (6) Harsingar.

Raginis of Raag Nat-Narayan-6

(1) Kamod (2) Kalyan (3) Abheri (4) Natki (5) Sarang (6) Nat Hamir.

The Putras of these Raginis are similar to the above mentioned two Mats except for a few minor differences. For example, according to Hanuman and Kallinatha Mat, Vidhvans, Kalyan and Sarang are mentioned as Putras, but these three are included among the Raginis in the Someshvar Mat. Vibhas is among the Putras according to Hanuman Mat, while it has been described as a Ragini in Someshvar Mat. In place of all these Raags, different names of Putras have been mentioned,

Bharat Mat

In the Bharat Mat six Raags have been described which are in accordance with the Hanuman Mat. These are : (1) Raag Bhairav (2) Raag Malkauns (3) Raag Hindol (4) Raag Deepak (5) Raag Shree (6) Raag Megh.

There are five Raginis and eight Putras of each Raag. In addition each Putra has been described to have a Bharya (wife). Following are the Raginis of each Raag.

Raginis of Raag Bhairav-5

(1) Madh Madhwi or Madhmad (2) Lalita (3) Berari (4) Bhairvi (5) Bohli, Bahuli or Bahul.

Raginis of Raag Malkauns-5

(1) Gauri (2) Dayavati (3) Todi (4) Khambhavati (5) Kukubh.

Raginis of Raag Hindol-5

(1) Ramkali (2) Mayavati (3) Asavari (4) Devari (5) Gunkali.

Raginis of Raag Deepak-5

(1) Kedaar (2) Gauri (3) Gaud (4) Gurjari (5) Rudravati or Rudrani.

Raginis of Raag Shree-5

(1) Saindhvi (2) Kafi (3) Thumri (4) Vichitra (5) Sirhati.

Raginis of Raag Megh-5

(1) Malhar (2) Sarang (3) Desi (4) Rati Ballabh (5) Kaveri.

According to Bharat Mat following are the Putras and their Bharyas (wives).

Putras of Raag Bhairav-8

(1) Devsakh (2) Lalit (3) Harsh (4) Madhav (5) Bilawal (6) Bengal (7) Vibhas (8) Pancham.

Bharyas-8

(1) Suha (2) Bilawali (3) Sorathi (4) Kumbhari (5) Andohi (6) Bahul Gujari (7) Pat Manjari (8) Bhairvi.

Putras of Raag Malkauns-8

(1) Gandhara (2) Shuddh (3) Makar or Mukar (3) Trichhana or Tiruchhana (5) Sahara (6) Shakti Ballabh (7) Mali Gaura (8) Kamod.

Bharyas-8

(1) Dhanashri (2) Malshri (3) Jaitshri (4) Sughrai (5) Durga (6) Gandhari (7) Bhimpalasi (8) Kamodi.

Putras of Raag Hindol-8

(1) Basant (2) Malwa (3) Maruv (4) Kushal (5) Bakhar Baral or Bikhar (6) Lank Dahan (7) Nag Dhwani (8) Dhol.

Bharyas-8

(1) Leelavati (2) Kairvi (3) Chaiti (4) Purbi (5) Parvati (6) Trivin (7) Devgiri (8) Saraswati.

Putras of Raag Deepak-8

(1) Kusum (2) Tunk (3) Nat-Narayan (4) Bhagra (5) Farodast (6) Rahas Mangala (7) Mangla Shatak (8) Adano or Adana.

Bharyas-8

(1) Mangal Gujari (2) Jaijaiwanti (3) Mal Gujari (4) Bhopali (5) Manohar (6) Ahiri (7) Yaman (8) Hamir.

Putras of Raag Rag Shree-8

(1) Shri Ravan (2) Kolahal (3) Sawant (4) Shankarvan or Shankar (5) Rakesar (6) Shat Raag (7) Vidhvans (8) Des Kar.

Bharyas-8

(1) Vijaya (2) Dhyanjai (3) Kumbh (4) Sohni (5) Sharad (6) Khem (7) Shashi Rekha (8) Sursati.

Putras of Raag Megh-8

(1) Kalayar (2) Bagesri (3) Shahana (4) Puriya (5) Kanhra (6) Tilak (7) Stambh (8) Shankarabharana.

Bharyas-8

(1) Karnatak (2) Kadvi (3) Kadamnat (4) Pahadi (5) Manjh (6) Paraj (7) Natmanjari (8) Shuddha Nath.

The author has clearly stated that some of the names of various Raags, which have been given in Tohfat-ul-Hind, are different names given in the ancient Shastric texts. For example, during authors' time Raag Karnati was called Kanhra. About Raag Kafi the author feels that earlier it might have been called Raag Kaphi, but after Muslim invasions its name might have been changed to Raag Kafi. It is quite interesting to note that Thumri has been describad as a Raag, was popular in the eastern parts of Uttar Pradesh. While describing Shuddha, Chhayalag and Sankeerna, the author has said that during his time some people were of the opinion that all the Raags were Shuddha and Raginis and their Putras were Sankeerna.

The formation of Sankeerna Raags has been described in great detail. The following 150 Raags have been included among Sankeerna Raags :

(1) Shuddha Nat (2) Kanhra Nat (3) Kedara Nat (4) Ahiri Nat (5) Hamir Nat (6) Kamod Nat (7) Sarang Nat (8) Chhana Nat (9) Nat Narayan (10) Kadam Nat (11) Baldaev (12) Raj Narayan (13) Kamod (14) Shuddha Kamod (15) Kalyan Kamod or Kalyan Vinod (16) Savant Kamod (17) Tilak Kamod (18) Bageshri (19) Shahana (20) Dana (21) Puriya (22) Shuddha Kalyan (23) Hamir or Gaurinath (24) Yaman (25) Khem Kalyan (26) Jaitkalyan (27) Dhanshri (28) Malshri (29) Jaitshri (30) Dhawalshri (31) Shat Raag (32) Saurashtak (33) Gunkali (34) Kumbhari (35) Madhmad (36) Saraswati (37) Vidhvans (38) Lank Dhwani (39) Shakti Ballabh (40) Shankar-abharana (41) Farodast (42) Pat Manjari (43) Devsakh (44) Bilawali (45) Kamod (46) Kamodi (47) Parvati (48) Bhim-palasi (49) Rambhavati (50) Gandhari (51) Berari (52) Bhagra (53) Leelavati (54) Manohar (55) Manohar Gauri (56) Tunk (57) Nag Dhwani (58) Abheri or Aheri (59) Rahas Mangal (60) Rajhans (61) Shri Samodh (62) Desi (63) Aansi or Hansi (64) Devgiri (65) Kolahal (66) Shri Ra-vana (67) Kukubh (68) Devari (69) Gujari (70) Mangal Gujri (71) Mal Gujari (72) Vichitra (73) Trivin (74) Kalai (Sughrai) (75) Shree Raag (76) Kedara (77) Hindol (78) Megh (79) Basant (80) Shankarvan (81) Bahul Gujari (82) Bhairvi (83) Bohli (84) Vibhas (85) Harsh (86) Madhav (87) Bengal (88) Lalit (89) Pancham (90) Suhu (91) Sorath (92) Gauri (93) Malkauns (94) Todi (95) Khambhavati (96) Tripchhana (97) Mali Gaura (98) Durga (99) Malawati (100) Malwa (101) Marwa (102) Bhankhar (103) Kairvi or Bhairvi (104) Jai Jaiwanti (105) Rudrani (106) Deepak (107) Gaud (108) Mangala Shatak (109) Jai Jaiwanti (110) Bhopali (111) Kafi (112) Thumri (113) Sursari (114) Sawant (115) Rakesar (116) Vijaya (117) Kumbh (118) Sharad (119) Khem (120) Shashi Rekha (121) Malhar (122) Sarang (123) Gaura (124) Deskar (125) Lalit (126) Chaiti (127) Mangal-Shatak (128) Rati Ballabh (129) Kalayar (130) Stambh (131) Kirman (132) Kadvi or Kaveri (133) Manjh or Manjha (134) Paraj (135) Nat Manjari (136) Gunkali (137) Triveni (138) Preeti (139) Kantha (140) Madh Madhvi (141) Kram Pancham (142) Sphurti (143) Saindhvi or Sindura (144) Marwa (145) Kala Pravin (146) Deepavati (147) Anup Roop (148) Chaiti Gauri (149) Gaud Sarang (150) Kapar Gauri.

In the author's opinion, majority of musicians during his time considered Deepak Raag as a Shuddha Raag with which no other Raag could be combined. Some others felt that Sarang, Kanhra, Gujari, Nat, Malhar, Todi and Gauri were the Shuddha Raags. According to some of the musicians, following are the Salang Raags :

(1) Deshkar (2) Vibhas (3) Lalit (4) Rewa (5) Bilawal (6) Megh (7) Sorath (8) Dhanashri (9) Gaura (10) Shree Raag (11) Deepak (12) Kafi (13) Kedaar.

In the chapter of Raag Adhyay a list of those Raags is given which were invented by some of the famous learned musicians.

Raags innovated by Amir Khusrau are the following :

(1) **Muhaiyar** : This Raag is based on Raag Gara and a Persian Muqam. According to another opinion, it is a combination of Todi and Usshaq.

(2) **Sazgiri** : It is a combination of Purvi, Gauri, Gunkali and a Persian Muqam.

(3) **Yamam** : It is a combination of Hindol and a Persian Muqam.

(4) **Usshaq** : For making this Raag, a Persian Muqam is combined with Sarang and Basant.

(5) **Muafiq** : It is also called Devali. It is an outcome of the combination of Todi, Malshri, Durga and Husseini.

(6) **Ghanam** : It has been composed through some alterations in Raag Purvi.

'7) **Farghan** : It is also called Farghana. It is a combination of Gunkali and Gaura.

(8) **Sarparda** : It is also called Surparda and it has been constructed by combining Gaud Sarang with a Persian Muqam.

(9) **Bakharz** : It is a combination of Deshkar and a Persian Muqam.

(10) **Farodast** : It is a combination of Raag Kanhra, Purvi, Gauri, Shyam and a Persian Muqam.

(11) **Sanam** : It is a combination of Kalyan and a Persian Muqam. Some people identify it as Nairez.

There is a description of 17 Raags innovated by Sultan Husain Sharqui in which there are 12 varieties of Shyam, 4 varieties of Todi and one variety of Asavari.

Following are the Raags comp᠀sed by Bahauddin Zakariya

and few other famous musicians : (1) Multani Dhanashri—A combination of Todi and Dhanashri. (2) Puriya Dhanashri—A combination of Puriya and Dhanashri. (3) Bahaduri Todi—A combination of Todi and Deshkar. (Nayak Bakshoo was the originator or this Raag). (4) Nayaki Kanhra—A combination of Kanhra, Shyam and Kumbh. (5) Nayaki Kalyan. (6) Jogiya Asavari. (7) Darbari Kanhra—This Raag was innovated by Tansen through a combination of Kanhra, Malhar and Kalyan.

A detailed description of Persian Muqams and their resemblance with the Indian Raags is given.

Tal Adhyay

This chapter has also been dealt with comprehensively. In the first Section the meaning and importance of Tal are given. The second Section deals with the Matras of different Talas. The third Section dwells upon the sequence of Talas. In the fourth Section, nine types of Nrityas (dances) have been discussed as given below : (1) Tandav (2) Lasya (3) Cheen (4) Shuddha Ang (5) Sulabh (6) Urp and Tirip (7) Shuddha Mudra (8) Lag-Dant (9) Dhilang.

In the fifth Section instruments have been classified into four categories : (1) Tat (2) Vitat (3) Ghan (4) Shikhar.

In the last part of Tal Adhyay, the different varieties of Taal have been discussed in great detail. Ninety two varieties of Taal, which were popular and practised during the author's time, have been thoroughly discussed. Names of these Taals are given below :

(1) Kokila (2) Raj Vidha Dhar Tal (3) Jaimahak (4) Tikamod (5) Vijayanand Tal (6) Krida Tal (7) Jaishri Tal (8) Makrand Tal (9) Krivritt Tal (10) Shree Krivitt Tal (11) Bhadra Mali Tal (12) Sam Tal (13) Nandan Tal (14) Mathka Tal (15) Bamathka Tal (16) Deepak Dhruva Tal (17) Uday Tal (18) Dhendki Tal (19) Visham Tal (20) Mall Tal (21) Purna Kangal Tal (22) Khand Kangal (23) Sam Kangal (24) Visham Kangal (25) Aidwan Tal (26) Chitra Tal (27) Jhamp Tal (28) Abhang Tal (29) Basant Tal (30) Pratap Shikhar (31) Jai Jhampal Tal (32) Chitramukh Tal (33) Madan Tal (34) Rat Tal (35) Parvati Lochan Tal (36) Leela Tal (37) Karna Tal (38) Lalit Tal (39) Raj Narayan Tal (40) Lakshmi Ish Tal (41) Lalit Priya Tal (42) Shree Nand Tal (43) Janak or Chanak Tal (44) Pradhan Tal (45) Raag Pradhan Tal (46)

Khat Tal (47) Antar Krida Tal (48) Bilokat Tal (49) Gaj Tal (50) Barna Jat Tal (51) Hans Tal (52) Karna Tal (53) Saras Tal (54) Chand Tal (55) Chandrakala Tal (56) Amiy Tal (57) Shikhand Tal (58) Ugra Tali Tal or Rudra Tali Tal (59) Mohna Tal (60) Dand Tal (61) Kumand Tal (62) Kovid Tal (63) Kuldheen Tal (64) Gauri Tal (65) Raj Nirgang Tal (66) Raj Mardand Tal (67) Nishank Tal (68) Sarangdev Tal (69) Ektali Tal (70) Gandak Tal (71) Math Vritta Tal (72) Nishank Leela Tal (73) Bramha Tal (74) Chitra Tal (75) Lubdha Tal (76) Rupak Tal (77) Isht Tal (78) Shankh Tal (79) Prat Tal (80) Sunj Tal (81) Sammukh Trital (82) Ishtalika Tal (83) Gaund Tal (84) Anang Tal (85) Abhinand Tal (86) Raihaiko (not clear) Tal (87) Karogi Tal (88) Varna Mukh Tal (89) Nayandi Tal (90) Davanal Tal (91) Bhagna Tal (92) Sursati Abhran Tal.

The study of Tohfat-ul-Hind as described in this chapter demonstrates that it is a very comprehensive and thorough work on the theory of Hindustani Music. The explanation on theory is lucid and various Raags and Raginis have been described with great clarity compared to Raag Darpan. Raag Darpan has lesser clarity in the description of Raags and presentation of the theory, probably because it is a translation of Man-Kautuhal in which the author has not been able to contribute his own understanding of music. On the other hand, in Tohfat-ul-Hind we find that the author has expressed his own knowledge of the theory, which reflects his deeper understanding and study of music.

Anothor distinctive feature of Tohfat-ul-Hind is a detailed chapter on Talas, which is not given in such details in the other works. The author has, however, not given description of the musicians of his time unlike Raag Darpan which contains such descriptions in detail.

CHAPTER III

Usulun-Naghmat-e-Asifi

NAGHMAT-E-ASIFI has been often described by the modern Indian musicologists as an important source of information on several significant aspects of Indian music. It is generally believed that Naghmat-e-Asifi was written by Mohammad Reza of Patna, and it deals with some of the highly useful features of Hindustani Music, especially the subject of classification of Raags. It is said that Reza disagreed with the system of Raag-Ragini-Putra classification of his time, and he wanted to introduce a new system for classifying Raags which would be based on some basic scientific principles. He criticized all the four Matas which were current during his time, and declared them out of date. Following are the opinions of few of our well known musicologists regarding this book.

According to Raja Nawab Ali, author of Maarifun-Naghmat, "Naghmat-e-Asifi was a highly useful scholarly book in Persian, which is not available these day".[1]

Herbert A. Popley states: "It was written by Mohammad Reza, a noble man of Patna. It is a critical work on Northern Indian music. He pronounces the various northern systems of classification to be out of date and has no use for the Raag-Ragini-Putra basis upon which it is built. He gives a new system of his own which brings together into groups of Raags which have similar features. This work is the first authority to take the Bilawal scale as its Shuddha scale. The author tells us that he wrote the book after consulting the best artistes available in his days. It is said that his Raag Lakshanas (definitions) are still in use by Hindustani Musicians."[2]

1. See Ali, R.N. : Maarifun-Naghmat.
2. Popley, Herbert A : Music of India; p. 21.

In the opinion of Rashid Malik: "With the changing environment and the acceptance of its new requirements, our scholars also started giving serious thought to music. Naghmat-e-Asifi is the first book which inspired the scholars to think on these lines and motivated them to concentrate on the subject of music in an appropriate manner. Setting aside commonly accepted works for the first time the author of Naghmat-e-Asifi has established the scale of Raag Bilawal as the Shuddha scale and criticised the four Matas, for the classification of Raags. According to him there should be some common factors between the Svaras of Raags and the Svaras of their Raginis. Keeping this principle in view he attempted to develop a new basis for classifying Raags and Raginis"[1]

Among the modern musiocologists Pandit V.N. Bhatkhande has given a great deal of thought to this work and has described it as one of the most informative and interesting works on music. In the first All-India Conference which was held in Baroda in 1916 he delivered a speech and expressed his ideas about this book in the following words :

"About the Fasli year 1224 (corresponding with A.D. 1813) one Mohammad Reza (a nobleman from Patna, according to Raja S.M. Tagore) wrote his work called Naghmat-e-Asifi. Reza seems to have been throughly dissatisfied with the absurd and meaningless Raag-Ragini-Putra classifications of his time, and took into his head to introduce some sort of intelligent principle in them. He boldly criticised all the four Matas (viz. Bharat Mata, Kallinatha Mata, Hanuman Mata and Someshvar Mata) wrongly respected in his time and pronounced them, as entirely out of date and unsuited to the spirit and practice of the times, and then laid down his own Mata. The great principle which he clearly enunciated for Raag-Ragini classifications was that there should be some similarity or common features between the Raag and its Raginis. Nobody will deny that his own classification does show that he acted upto his principle. Reza was no doubt a talented musician. I wish we had men of this type now. I shall here draw your attention to one or two points is connection with this work which will be of some historical importance to us. In the Naghmat-e-Asifi for the first time, do we come across a reli-

1. Malik, Rashid : Hazrat Amir Khusrau Ka Ilm-e-Mousiqui Au Doosre Maqalat; pp. 112-114.

able authority with the Bilawal scale for its Shuddha scale. Naghmat was written, it appears, in the time of Asafuddaullah, the Nawab of Oudh. The author tells us that he wrote the book after fully consulting all the available best artistes of the day. Probably in a conference under the Presidentship of the Nawab many of the Raag definitions of Naghmat will be found useful even at this day by our Hindustani musicians."[1]

It may be noted from the foregoing discussions that there are two titles, namely, Naghmat-e-Asifi and Usulum-Naghmat-e-Asifi, which apparently refer to the same manuscript. The question, therefore, arises whether the correct title of the concerned manuscript is Naghmat-e-Asifi or Usulun-Naghmat-e-Asifi, or whether one of these two titles refers to the summary of the original manuscript. A search of all the possible sources of manuscripts has indicated that the original manuscript of Naghmat-e-Asifi is not traceable. It may be recalled that Raja Nawab Ali had also referred to the non-availability of the manuscript.

Pandit V.N. Bhatkhande in his speech which was delivered in Baroda Conference has given a clue regarding this manuscript. While discussing about the book he mentioned that the President of that Conference procured a copy of this book and he was going to present it to the Conference.[2] At the same time it is worthy of note that whatever matter and contents of Naghmat-e-Asifi have been described by Pandit V.N. Bhatkhande and few other musicians, are also traceable in the book named Usulun-Naghmat-e-Asifi. For example, the subject of Shuddha Thaat has been clearly described in Usulun-Naghmat-e-Asifi, and it has been mentioned that Bilawal is the Shuddha Thaat of our musical system.[3] Similarly, the author has written his own Mata also in this book.

Rashid Malik who has given a comprehensive description of this work in his book "Hazrat Amir Khusrau Ka Ilm-e-Mousiqui Aur Doosre Maqalat", has given the name of the

1. A Short Historical Survey of the Music of Upper India (A reproduction of speech delivered by Pt. V.N. Bhatkhande at the first All India Music Conference at Baroda in 1916).
2. Pt. V.N. Bhatkhande, A Short Historical Survey of the Music of Upper India.
3. Usulun-Naghmat-e-Asifi, Manuscript p. 31.

manuscript as Usulun-Naghmat-e-Asifi.[1] In this way the following possibilities emerge from the above discussion: either Naghmat-e-Asifi and Usulun-Naghmat-e-Asifi are two different titles of the same manuscript, or the original manuscript, the title of which was Naghmat-e-Asifi has been copied by the scribes who gave it the title 'Usulun-Naghmat-e-Asifi'. Another possibility is that Usulun-Naghmat-e-Asifi is the summarized version of the original work and retains the basic principles enunciated in it.

Another point on which there is difference of opinion is the name of the author of the work. Mohammed Reza is considered to be the author of this book according to Pandit V.N. Bhatkhande and other modern musicologists. However, the name of the author given in the manuscript entitled Usulun-Naghmat-e-Asifi is Ghulam Reza Bin Mohammad Panah. Rashid Malik in his Urdu book has stated the author's name as Ghulam Reza instead of Mohammad Reza[2]. The manuscript which has been utilized as the basis for this work has Ghulam Reza's name as the author in the introduction of the manuscript. Whereas at the end of the manuscript the following statement is given :

"The writer of Usulun-Naghmat-e-Asifi is Sabir Ali Shah. This manuscript has been copied from the documents obtained from Hasan Maududi Al Kumhari. The copying of this manuscript has been completed on Saturday the 8th of Rabi-ul-Awwal in Hijri 1309. The scribe of this manuscript is Mohammad Ali Bin Syed Barkhurdar Ali Bin Syed Abbas Ali, resident of Mohalla Darbar Kalan, Amroha (U.P.)"[3]

Regarding the year of writing of Naghmat-e-Asifi there is lack of clarity. According to general belief this book was written in the year 1813 A.D. But a perusal of the various manuscripts of Usulun-Naghmat-e-Asifi indicates that this book might have been written a few years earlier.

Having examined the various questions regarding the name

1. Malik, R: Hazrat Khusrau Ka Ilm-e-Mousiqui Aur Doosre Maqalat; p. 112.
2. Malik, R : Hazrat Amir Khusrau Ka Ilm-e-Mousiqui Aur Doosre Maqalat, p. 112.
3. Usulun-Naghmat-e-Asifi; Manuscript at Delhi University, p. 145

of the book, name of the author and the date of its writing, we may now examine the contents of Usulun-Naghmat-e-Asifi. The main points of the book are given below in a summarized form.

The first few pages are devoted to the glory of God. After that there is mention of the author's name and the purpose of his writing this book. The author has given the following description :

"Nawab Asafuddaullah asked Ghulam Reza Bin Mohammad Panah to write a book on the subject of Music based on the old Indian Sanskrit books, keeping the standards which were maintained by the earlier Indian philosophers. Although the books on this subject were rarely available, and for many years nobody had written a reliable book, nor the contemporary musicians were interested in discussing the subject of musicology, yet I engaged myself in writing this book according to the directions of the Nawab. Whatever discussions I had with the Nawab on this subject from time to time has been included in this book. Besides, I obtained useful information from Khwaja Hassan Maududi Al Kumhari (a Sufi saint who was alive at that time), and several other well-known contemporary artistes. Further, I also compiled the points from the best available books, and thus I composed a small volume which I have named 'Usulun-Naghmat-e-Asifi'.[1].

The book contains following six Asala (chapters) : I. Svar Adhyay II. Raag Adhyay III. Srakeerna Adhyay IV. Prabandha Adhyay V. Taal Adhyay VI. Vadya Adhyay.

The writer has mentioned about three other chapters, namely : Arth Adhyay, Nritya Adhyay and Bhav Adhyay, which according to him were not in vogue during his time and, therefore, he has excluded them. Following is a brief summary of each chapter :

I. Svar Adhyay

It is based on eighteen Fasals (sections) : (1) Description of Awaz (voice) (2) Description of Nad (3) Description of Svara (4) Description of Svar and Shruti (5) Shuddha and Ashuddha Svara (6) Shruti (7) Vikrit Svara (8) The importance of Svara and Shruti (9) Tivra and Komal Svaras (10)

1. Raza, Ghulam : Usulun-Naghmat-e-Asifi; p. 7.

Five Jatis of Shrutis (11) Vadi Svara (12) Gram (13) Murchhana (14) Archek (15) Tana (16) The seven Svaras and their origin according to various philosophers (17) Varna, (18) Alankar.

II. Raag Adhyay

This is the most noteworthy chapter of this book. A detailed study of this chapter will be highly useful even for modern musicologists. In this chapter the author has for the first time challenged and criticized the four Matas of his time and has brought to surface the defects of the Raag-Raginis system for classifying Raags. Along with it he has also given his own system which provided a new direction for classifying Raags. In this chapter, for the first time Bilawal has been identified as Shuddha Thaat, whereas there is no mention of the same in the two earlier famous books, namely: Tohfat-ul-Hind and Raag Darpan. The Thaat system of classifying Raags, which is widely accepted and prevalent today, has some resemblance with the system described in Usulun-Naghmat-e-Asifi. There are four sections in this chapter : (1) Appreciation of Geet (2) Raags and Raginis (3) Description of four Matas (5) Tana-Prastar

III. Prakeerna Adhyay

It is based on six sections : (1) Alphabets of Alap (2) Four Sthanas of Alap (3) Varieties of Alap (4) Gamak (5) Classification of musicians (6) The qualities and defects of musicians.

IV. Prabandha Adhyay

This chapter is about the different varieties of Geet.

V. Tal Adhyay

It deals with the details of those Tals which were popular during the author's time.

VI. Vadya Adhyay

It gives a concise description of classification of Indian instruments.

Following is a detailed account of the above mentioned chapters :

I. Svar Adhyay

This chapter contains most of the points which have already been covered in Tohfat-ul-Hind and Raag Darpan. It may be noted here that these points appear to have been translated from the origiaal Sanskrit books. However, the author's description about Shruti and Svara is very lucid and clear. The writer says that all the ancient writers (Shiva, Mahabat, Durga, Narad, Someshvar, Kallinatha, Bharata, Hanuman, Ha-Ha, and Hu-Hu) are of the opinion that there is not much difference between Shruti and Svara. But he further says that if we accept this viewpoint, then the questions arise why should there be a division between the two, and why are these two terminologies utilized? The author offers his own response to these questions by stating that Svara and Shruti are the same phenomena, but the difference lies in listening to them. In other words, out of the 22 Shrutis those which can be heard are Svaras, and remaining which are inaudible are called Shrutis. For example, river and the stream are one and the same, and yet they have two different names.

The writer further says that Narad has given twenty two names of Shrutis : (1) Tivra (2) Kumudvati (3) Manda (4) Chhandovati (5) Dayavati (6) Raktika (7) Ranjani (8) Rudra (9) Krodha (10) Vajrika (11) Prasadini (12) Parvat (13) Marjani (14) Kchhati (15) Rakta (16) Sandipni (17) Alapini (18) Madanti (16) Rambha (20) Rohini (21) Ugra (22) Kshobhini.

A distinct point which deserves attention here is that two new names, Parvat and Rambha, have been mentioned in place of Preeti and Ramya respectively, unlike the well established names of Shrutis.

Vikrit Svara

Vikrit refers to deviation of the sounds from their original places. The source of these Vikrit Svaras (Komal and Tivra) are the Shrutis. There are twelve names of Vikrit Svaras :

1. Kshat—In this Rishabh takes one Shruti from Shadaja.

2. Akshat—When Rishabh takes two Shrutis from Shadaja, it is called Akshat.

3. Kakuli—Gandhar takes one Shruti from Rishabh in Kakuli.

4. Ati Kakuli—When Gandhar takes two Shrutis from Rishabh it is called Ati Kakuli.

5. Nandli—Madhyam takes one Shrtuti from Gandhar.

6. Ati Nandli—Madhyam takes two Shrutis from Gandhar. But Gandhar consists of only two Shrutis, that is why in some

Matas, Gandhar contains three Shrutis and Gandhar remains stable on its third Shruti.

7. Vikrit—In this Pancham takes one Shruti from Madhyam.

(8) Ati Vikrit—Pancham takes two Shrutis from Madhyam in Ati Vikrit.

(9) Antar—In this Dhaivat takes two Shrutis from Pancham.

(10) Bahu Antar—In this Nishad takes two Shrutis from Pancham.

(11) Kaishik—In this Nishad takes one Shruti from Dhaivat.

12. Ati Kaishik—In this Nishad takes two Shrutis from Dhaivat.

According to another classification, Vikrit Svaras are of the following six types : (1) Tivra (2) Tivratar (3) Tivratam (4) Komal (5) Ati Komal (6) Sukari.

There are five Jatis of Shrutis : (1) Deepta (2) Ayta (3) Karuna (4) Mirdha or Mridu (5) Madhya.

Regarding Gram, the author says that in our old Shastras three types of Grams have been described—(1) Shadaj Gram (2) Madhyam Gram (3) Gandhar Gram. The author has, however, pointed out that in his period the musicians could not practice this systems. He further states that two Grams, Shadaja and Madhyam, could be recited only by a few musicians. But neither the vocalists nor the instrumentalists of that time could perform the Gandhar Gram. Later the author emphasizes that these three Grams have a considerable influence on the Thaat system.[1] In his opinion the essence of Gram is to obtain Svar-Samvad. He has also given examples of the above mentioned Grams :

Pa Dha Ni Sa Re Ga Ma Pa—First Gram.
Pa Ma Ga Re Sa Ni Dha Pa I
Sa Ni Dha Pa Ma Ga Re Sa Second Gram
Ma Ga Re Sa Ni Dha Pa Ma I
Ga Re Sa Ni Dha Pa Ma Ga Third Gram

In accordance with the above system sometimes Pancham

1. Usulun-Naghmat-e-Asifi p. 31.

becomes Rishabh, and Rishabh becomes Pancham; Gandhar becomes Dhaivat, and Dhaivat becomes Gandhar; Madhyam becomes Nishad and Nishad becomes Madhyam; Pancham becomes Madhyam and Madhyam becomes Pancham.

The above description of Gram is not very clear. It seems that the scribe of the book has not written few references from the original work. Therefore, it is very difficult to understand the above mentioned description of Svar-Samvad.

The author has illustrated this system through a diagram.[1]

Sa	Re	Ga	Ma	Pa	Dha	Ni
Ni	Sa	Re	Ga	Ma	Pa	Dha
Dha	Ni	Sa	Re	Ga	Ma	Pa
Pa	Dha	Ni	Sa	Re	Ga	Ma
Ma	Pa	Dha	Ni	Sa	Re	Ga
Ga	Ma	Pa	Dha	Ni	Sa	Re
Re	Ga	Ma	Pa	Dha	Ni	Sa

Murchhana

Murchhana refers to the expression of Svaras, and is based on Grams. Every Gram consists of seven Murchhanas. Two principles are popular for deriving Murchhanas. For example, the Murchhanas of first Gram which starts from Mandra-Sthan can be divided into two folllowing methods :

First Method

(1) Uttar Mandra —Sa Re Ga Ma Pa Dha Ni
Ni Dha Pa Ma Ga Re Sa

(2) Ranjani —Ni Sa Re Ga Ma Pa Dha
Dha Pa Ma Ga Re Sa Ni

(3) Uttaraita —Dha Ni Sa Re Ga Ma Pa
Pa Ma Ga Re Sa Ni Dha

(4) Shuddha Shadaja —Pa Dha Ni Sa Re Ga Ma
Ma Ga Re Sa Ni Dha Pa

(5) Machhari Karta —Ma Pa Dha Ni Sa Re Ga
Ga Re Sa Ni Dha Pa Ma

(6) Ashva-Kanta —Ga Ma Pa Dha Ni Sa Re
Re Sa Ni Dha Pa Ma Ga

(7) Abhirudgata —Re Ga Ma Pa Dha Ni Sa
Sa Ni Dha Pa Ma Ga Re

Second Method

(1) Sa Re Ga Ma Pa Dha Ni — Ni Dha Pa Ma Ga Re Sa

1. Usuln-Naghmat-e-Asifi, p. 33.

(2) Re Ga Ma Pa Dha Ni Sa — Sa Ni Dha Pa Ma Ga Re
(3) Ga Ma Pa Dha Ni Sa Re — Re Sa Ni Dha Pa Ma Ga
(4) Ma Pa Dha Ni Sa Re Ga — Ga Re Sa Ni Dha Pa Ma
(5) Pa Dha Ni Sa Re Ga Ma — Ma Ga Re Sa Ni Dha Pa
(6) Dha Ni Sa Re Ga Ma Pa — Pa Ma Ga Re Sa Ni Dha
(7) Ni Sa Re Ga Ma Pa Dha — Dha Pa Ma Ga Re Sa Ni

Murchhanas of Madhyam Gram

(1) Suri or Sauveri (2) Haranaswadh (3) Kalopita (4) Shuddha Madhya (5) Margi (6) Purbi (7) Prakharka.

Murchhanas of Gandhar Gram

(1) Veda (2) Vishala (3) Sumukhi (4) Vistarika (5) Roopi (6) Prokta (7) Anta or Alapta.

Raag Jati and Tana

Jatis of Raags are divided into three parts : (1) Avdav (2) Shadav (3) Sampurna.

Tana

Chapter on Tanas has been written in great detail. In the beginning of the chapter four types of Tanas are described :

(1) Archek—Example—Sa Sa
(2) Ghatak[1]—Example—Sa Re Sa Re Sa
(3) Samak—Example—Sa Re Ga Ga Re Sa
(4) Svaramak—Example—Sa Re Ga Ma —Ma Ga Re Sa

In Hindustani Music the act of stretching, magnifying and splitting is known as Koot Tana and Prastar. Koot Tana can be produced in five thousand and forty different ways. Such as, striking on Svara would make one Tana. For example — Sa, Sa. If one Svara is combined with another, it will make two Tanas. If above two Svaras are combined with the third Svara, it would lead to the formation of six Tanas. For example —(1) Sa, Re, Ga, (2) Re, Sa, Ga, (3) Sa, Ga, Re (4) Ga, Sa, Re (5) Re, Ga, Sa (6) Ga, Re, Sa. If these six Svaras are combined with the fourth Svara, it will result in 24 Tanas. For example :

(1) Sa Re Ga Ma (2) Re Sa Ga Ma
(3) Sa Ga Re Ma (4) Ga Sa Re Ma
(5) Re Ga Sa Ma (6) Ga Re Sa Ma
(7) Sa Re Ga Ma (8) Re Sa Ma Ga
(9) Sa Ma Re Ga (10) Ma Sa Re Ga

1. Ghatak, Samakand, Svaramak have been mentioned as Gatik, Samik and Svarantar respectively in Sangeet Ratnakar.

(11) Re Ma Sa Ga (12) Ma Re Sa Ga
(13) Sa Ga Ma Re (14) Ga Sa Ma Re
(15) Sa Ma Ga Re (16) Ma Sa Ga Re
(17) Ga Ma Sa Re (18) Ma Ga Sa Re
(19) Re Ga Ma Sa (20) Ga Re Ma Sa
(21) Re Ma Ga Sa (22) Ma Re Ga Sa
(23) Ga Ma Re Sa (24) Ma Ga Re Sa

In the same way, the moving up from the fourth to the fifth Svara will create one hundred and twenty Tanas, and multiplying the sixth Svara with the last Svara would give five thousand and forty Tanas.

Varna and Alankar

Varna means colour. The author states that according to some Unani (Greek) philosohers, the seven Svaras of Saptak have been derived from the seven heavenly bodies in the universe, and each has taken the Varna (colour) of that particular heavenly body. Such as Shadaja has taken its colour from the moon, Rishabh has taken its colour from Mercury. Gandhar Svara is affected by Zohra (Venus), Madhyam has taken the colour of sun, Pancham is influenced by Mirrikh (Mars), Dhaivat is influenced by Mushtari (Jupiter), and Nishad has been brought forth from Venus. In the same way names of various colours and the names of Svaras influenced by them are mentioned.

Svara	**Colour**
(1) Shadaja	— White, Red, Green, Black, Yellow
(2) Rishabh	— Blue
(3) Gandhar	— White
(4) Madhyam	— Orange
(5) Pancham	— Black
(6) Dhaivat	— White and Yellow
(7) Nishad	— Black

The author has skipped over the technical meaning of Varna and has discussed Alankar. The topic of Alankar is almost the translation of Parijat of Ahobal. Four types of Alankar along with their examples have been given (1) Sthai (2) Arohi (3) Avrohi (4) Sanchari

II. Raag Adhyay

This chapter has been divided into two parts :

First part—In this part the qualities of musicians have

been described. In this connection four parts of Geet have been mentioned. These have been called the Angas (limbs). It has been further stated that a good musician must be familiar with these four Angas : (1) Ragaang (2) Bhashaang (3) Kriyaang (4) Upaang

Second part—In this section the author has discussed comprehensively the Raag-Ragini system of his time. Raags are classified in three categories—(1) Shudda (2) Salang, and lastly, (3) Sankeerna.

Further, the author states that in his period Shuddha Raags were not very popular but Salang and Sankeerna Raags were very much in vogue and musicians of his period were making various experiments by combining several Raags and innovating new Sankeerna Raags.

In Usulun-Naghmat-e-Asifi, the description of four Matas (Somesvar, Kallinatha, Bharat, and Hanuman Mat) have been copied from the book Tohfat-ul-Hind. Referring to the 'Tohfat-ul-Hind' the author has elaborated these four Matas, and has mentioned that during his time Hanuman Mata was most widely accepted. The names of Raags and their Raginis are the same as given in Tohfat-ul-Hind, which have already been described earlier. The author has pointed out the deficiencies in the system of classifying Raags and Raginis and has given his own opinion also. Further, he states the structure of the Raags prevalent during his time were different from the Raags described in Tohfat-ul-Hind. For example, in the description of Raag Malkauns the writer states : "According to the writer of Tohfat-ul-Hind, Malkauns is a Raag of Sampurna Jati and all seven Svaras are used in this Raag, but in my opinion Raag Malkauns is a Raag of Avdav Jati, because only five Svaras are permissible in the Raag. In the present times this Raag is very popular, and none of the musicians would agree that it is a Raag of Sampurna Jati'.[1] In the same way he writes about Raag Bhairav : "According to Tohfat ul-Hind, Raag Bhairav is of Avdav Jati and only five Svaras, (Dha, Ni, Sa, Ga, Ma) can be used in it. But in my period Bhairav is accepted by all as Sampurna and all Svaras are used in this Raag".[2]

1. Usulun-Naghmat-e-Asifi, p. 55.
2. Usulun-Naghmat-e-Asifi, p. 54.

Classification of Raags according to Shams-ul-Aswat

According to a Persian book, Shams-ul-Aswat (Sun of Melodies), there are only three Raags and each Raag has six Raginis. In this way, according to this school of thought, there are three Raags and eighteen Raginis. Three main Raags have been taken from the above mentioned four Matas. Following is a concise description of this system:[1] (1) Raag Malkauns (2) Raag Hindol (3) Raag Deepak.

Raginis of Raag Malkauns-6

(1) Kanhra (2) Balkesari (3) Puriya
(4) Kumbhavan (5) Devsakhi (6) Sughrai

Raginis of Raag Hindol-6

(1) Yaman (2) Sughrai (3) Bhakhra
(4) Parji (5) Bhimpalasi (6) Sindura

Raginis of Raag Deepak-6

(1) Asavari (2) Kukubha (3) Abheri
(4) Saindhvi (5) Patmanjari (6) Manohar

Surprisingly, in the above classification, Raag Sughrai has been described as the Ragini of two Raags, viz., Raag Hindol and Raag Deepak. The author writes that this system of Shams-ul-Aswat is traceable in a few other books also.

Third part—The third part of Raag Adhyay is very significant, because in this part for the first time in the history of Hindustani music the author shows his disagreement with the system of Raag-Ragini, Putra and Bharya, which was popular in his time. He introduced a system of his own which is based on some scientific principles and is reasonably acceptable. He laid down his own Mata and expressed his view that in the classification of Raags there should be some similarity between the Raags and their Raginis, and in this attempt he was fairly successful. The writer says that he laid down his own Mata after consulting old Shastric texts and through discussions with the musicians and musicologists of his time.[2] In his classification he has successfully compared the Raginis with their Raags and indicated the similarities between them. According to his classification, following are the six Raags and their Raginis :

Raag	Raginis
(1) Bhairav	(1) Bhairavi (2) Ramkali (3) Gujari

1. Usulun-Naghmat-e-Asifi, p. 88.
2. Usulun-Naghmat-e-Asifi, p. 89,

(4) Khat (5) Gandhari (6) Asavari

(2) Malkauns — (1) Bageshwari (2) Todi (3) Desi (4) Suha (5) Sughrai (6) Multani

(3) Hindol — (1) Puriya (2) Basant (3) Lalit (4) Pancham (5) Dhanashri (6) Marwa

(4) Shree. — (1) Gauri (2) Purvi (3) Gaura (4) Trivin (5) Malshri (6) Jaitshri

(5) Megh — (1) Madhmad (2) Gaud (3) Shuddha Sarang (4) Barhans (5) Samant (6) Sorath

(6) Nat — (1) Chhayanat (2) Hamir (3) Kalyan (4) Kedar (5) Bihagda (6) Yaman

Notation System

In this portion of the book, the importance of writing music is emphasized, and the difficulties and complexities of this art have been pointed out. A brief description of the notation system prevalent during the writer's time has been given. At that time it was common practice to write the Geet and its meaning, before writing the notation.

Following are the other signatures of Notation :

(1) Svara of first Saptak
(2) Svara of Second Saptak
(3) Svara of third Saptak
(4) Shuddha Svara
(5) Tivra Svara
(6) Tivratar Svara
(7) Tivratam Svara
(8) Komal Svara
(9) Sikar Svara
(10) Akar
(11) Dhrut ½ Matra
(12) Laghu Svara 1 Matra
(13) Drut Viram 3/4 Matra
(14) Laghu Viram 1¼ Matra

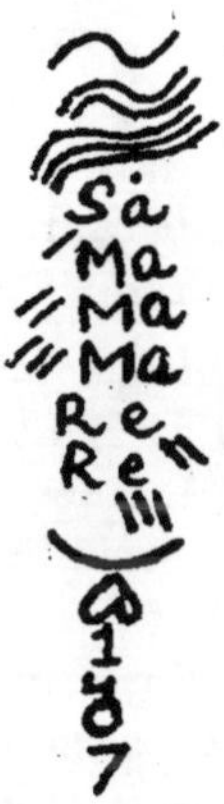

III. Prakeerna Adhyay

This chapter deals mainly with the topic of Anibaddha Gana. In this chapter the methods of singing Alap has been described in considerable detail. Four Sthanas or Sanchar of Alap have been mentioned which should be particularly kept in mind at the time of performing Alap : (1) Vadi—First Sanchar (2) Samvadi—Second Sanchar (3) Anuvadi—Third Sanchar (4) Vivadi—Fourth Sanchar.

First Sanchar deals with the Vadi Svar. Second Sanchar deals with the Samvadi Svar. Third Sanchar deals with the Anuvadi Svar. Fourth Sanchar deals with the Vivadi Svar.

Four types of Alap have been described :

(1) Ragalapti (2) Rupkalapti (3) Sam Alap (4) Thaynhi.

Twenty types of Gamak hava been described as given below : (1) Kampit (2) Ahat (3) Andolit (4) Purwahat (5) Uttarit (6) Prithpahat (7) Dorahat (8) Ashrat (9) Sannit (10) Tirip (11) Gharshana (12) Anavgharsh (13) Bansutthan (14) Ugra (15) Kartari (16) Sahat (17) Seemni (18) Dhal (19) Sudhal (20) Mudra.

After the topic of Gamak, different categories of musicians and their qualities have been discussed in detail. The topic of Vakgeykara (composer) has also been dealt with elaborately. But most of these parts are merely a translation from the previous books like Tohfat-ul-Hind and other Sanskrit works of that period.

IV. Prabandha Adhyay

This is a highly informative chapter, because different varieties of the forms of singing have been described in it. Some of these were popular during the author's time, and some could be found only in the Shastrik texts. According to the author, Nibaddha Gan is classified into two categories—(1) Margi (2) Desi.

Following varieties of Margi and Desi Sangeet are described : (1) Geet (2) Jhoomra (3) Suraj Prakash (4) Prabandha (5) Dhruva (6) Dhruvapad (7) Karsha (8) Bar (9) Bagdhar (10) Khyal (11) Tappa (12) Qaul (13) Farsi (14) Hori.

Among the above mentioned forms, Dhruvapad has been described comprehensively, and in the author's view, Dhruvapad can consist of five, four, three, two or one Tuks. The name of these parts are given as below : (1) Udgrah (2) Sthai (3) Melapak (4) Antara (4) Bhog (6) Dhruva.

It is interesting to note that the description of Dhruvapad is very similar to the structure of Prabandha form. A study of this part of the book reveals that Dhruvapad was the most widely prevalent form of singing during the author's time and Prabandha form had become extinct. Possibly, this was the period when Prabandha was beginning to be called Dhruvapad by the musicians, and gradually was totally merged in the Dhruvapad style of singing.

V. Taal Adhyay

The author has stated that whereas it is a large topic, he has given a brief account of it. He has given the names of various Talas which were practised during his time.

(1) Sadra (2) Khairabadi (3) Jangali (4) Ada Chautala (5) Ektala (6) Dheema Teen Tal (7) Sool Fakhta (8) Chautal (9) Shikhar Tal.

After the definition of Taal, the writer mentions the ten Pranas or rules of Talas elaborately. Following are the names of the ten Pranas :

(1) Kaal (2) Marg (3) Kriya (4) Ang (5) Graha (6) Jati (7) Kala (8) Laya (9) Jati (10) Prastar.

VI. Vadya Adhyay

This is the last chapter of the book. In this chapter definitions of the four categories of instruments have been given. This part of the book appears to have been copied from other books.

A detailed description of Been (Veena) player is given. It seems that Been was an important and popular instrument among the musicians during that time. Regarding the Been, at one place the author states : "The instrument named Been is often called by Hindus as Rudra Veena, and they believe that all pains and sufferings are removed by listening to Been.[1] The author further describes the twelve Lakshanas of Been players as given below :

(1) A Been player should be a cultured man having good tastes. (2) He should be clear hearted. (3) He should be a man of sound character. (4) He should not have a prejudiced mind. (5) He should possess long hands. (6) He should be one who sits erect. (7) He should be cheerful and should have good habits. (8) He should have the knowledge of Ragang, Bhashang and Upang. (9) He should be familiar with the different varieties of Gamak. (10) He should have a good command of Svaras. (11) He must understand the Graha and Murchhana thoroughly. (12) He should be hard working.

In the end of the book, the writer has written some auspicious and inauspicious alphabets which should or should not be used in the beginning of Khyal and Dhruvapad styles of singing..

1. Usulun-Naghmat-e-Asifi, p. 142.

The foregoing description and discussion leads us to the conclusion that Usulun-Naghmat-e-Asifi is a comprehensive work on music of the later part of the eighteenth century. The two main points which may be considered as the original contributions of this book are a new viewpoint on the systems of classification of Raags and Raginis, and treating Bilawal scale as the Shuddha scale. Thus the approach followed in this book is more or less similar to the Thaat system which is being followed by the musicians of the present time. While describing the Shrutis at one place, the author states that the interval between the Shrutis of Raag Beravar or Bilawal is the real Shuddha scale,[1] and this scale has considerable influence on the Thaat system. Although the author has not elaborated this point in detail, yet this is a significant point which has considerable significance for the modern scholars of music.

1. Usulur-Naghmat-e-Asifi, p. 29.

CHAPTER IV

Nadirat-e-Shahi and Other Manuscripts and Books

IN the foregoing chapters we have discussed in detail the three major manuscripts belonging to the seventeenth and eighteenth centuries. In this chapter, Nadirat-e-Shahi, which is also an important source of information regarding the forms and styles of music prevalent during that period, has been briefly described. In addition, ten other manuscripts and books pertaining to this period have also been briefly described to give a picture of the type of literature, development of Hindustani music and description of musicians during this period. The manuscripts and books selected for this purpose are : (1) Risala-e-Zikr-e-Mughannian-e-Hindustan (2) Parijatak (3) Kitab-e-Nauras (4) Sahas-Rasa (5) Mirat-e-Aftab Numa (6) Khulasat-ul-Aish Alam Shahi (7) Tashrih-ul-Mousiqui (8) Muftah-ul-Sarod (6) Marfat-ul-Naghm (10) Shams-ul-Aswat.

Nadirat-e-Shahi

Nadirat-e-Shahi is the collection of Shah Alam's Urdu, Persian, Hindi and Punjabi songs. This manuscript is available in Reza Library of Rampur. It was purchased by the Nawab of Rampur through Mirza Dagh Dehlvi. The manuscript has been published on behalf of the Reza Library of Rampur by Imtiaz Ali Khan Arshi. Arshi, a well known scholar of Urdu and Persian, has also written a detailed preface to the book.

An examination of the manuscript reveals that this is the same manuscript which was prepared for Shah Alam, because after each section of songs there are a couple of plain pages, which, according to Arshi, might have been left blank for adding more songs in due course.[1] Arshi has given following details

1. Imtiaz Ali Arshi : Nadirat-e-Shahi ; Preface ; p. 47.

about the life of Shah Alam.

Shah Alam was born during the reign of Mohammad Shah. His Islamic name was Mirza Abdullah and his family name was Ali Gauhar. He was often called Mirza Bulaqui and Lal Mian in his childhood.[1] His mother's name was Lal Kunwar.[2] But after his mother's death, he was adopted by Begum Zeenat Mahal. His father Azizuddin Alam Saani was arrested by Badshah Farrukh-Seer. Shah Alam was born on 14th June 1728 A.D., while his parents were in captivity.

Although by nature Shah Alam was a very kind hearted and courageous person, he lacked the ability to rule the state. He used to trust all the sycophants, and was pleasure-seeking and lazy during his youth. During his later years he spent most of his time in prayer and writing copies of the Holy Quran. He respected learned Sufis and saints. He had great admiration for Khwaja Moinuddeen Chishti and Sheikh Abdul Qadir. The 'Urs' of these saints were celebrated in a big way in the fort and during the 'Urs' the musical sittings of Sama (musical gatherings of Muslim saints) were very much in vogue. A great deal of money was given in charity on such occasions.[3] During his journeys he often visited the tombs (Mazars) of saints and used to perform Fatihas (holy rituals) there.[4]

He had a complete command of Persian, Urdu, Hindi and Punjabi languages, in poetry as well as in prose. He had some knowledge of Arabic, Sanskrit and Turkish languages also. He had good knowledge of the art of music, and he had indicated in Nadirat-e-Shahi that he was a disciple of Nazar Ali.[5] In 1704 A.D. his father Emadul-Mulk became the King of Delhi. Shah Alam was sent to Allahabad, where he stayed for about seven years. He spent most of his time in luxury and pleasure. Some of the undesirable company that he had during this period led to bad habits in him.[6] Later, he spent some time in Bihar, at Lucknow and Saharanpur. During these years he

1. Imtiaz Ali Arshi : Nadirat-e-Shahi ; Preface ; p. 5. Also see Waqyat-e-Azfari.
2. Waqyat-e-Azfari, p. 8.
3. Abe-Hayat ; p. 186.
4. Shah-Alam-Nama ; pp. 160, 117, 103, 69.
5. Nadirat-e-Shahi ; p. 43.
6. Taarikh-e-Hindustan : and Nadirat-e-Shahi, Preface, p. 17.

had several confrontations with Sikhs, Marathas and Jats. He then returned to Delhi.

Jagirdar Ghulam Qadir Khan (son of Zabta Khan), whom Shah Alam had defeated, and had also arrested his entire family, had not forgotten the earlier insult to him by Shah Alam. So he decided to attack Shah Alam and joined hands with Mughal soldiers. One day he called Shah Alam to the Diwan-e-Aam, and after overpowering him gouged out his eyes.

During his last few years, he was prisoner of Britishers, and he died in the year 1806 A.D. (1221 A.H.). He was buried near the grave of Bahadur Shah I, at the Qutab-Sahib.

The original manuscript is written on deep almond coloured Kashmiri paper in Devnagri and Urdu (Nastaleeq) script. It appears that the scribes of these two scripts were different persons, because at some points there are differences in the words chosen by them. The Geets (song) have been clustered together into several groups according to the subject and language.

At the end of the book there is a Hindi couplet, which indicates that this book was entitled Nadirat-e-Shahi. The couplet reads as follows :

मोद उपावे चित्त को, सबै रसन को घाम ।
'नादिरातेशाही' धर्यो या पौथी को नाम ।।

After this there is a Persian Rubai, which reveals that this book was written in the year 1797 A.D. (1212 A.H.), in accordance with the personal direction of Shah Alam. The Rubai reads as follows :

این نسخه که ہست جامع جملہ علوم
گردید بحکم شاہِ عالم مرقوم
اثنا عشر از احاد ہم بود مائته
کیں گشت بنادرات شاہی موسوم

The songs of Nadirat-e-Shahi (except a few) have been composed in Raag and Taal, and their names have been given at the beginning of each song. Since his mother was a Hindu lady, Shah Alam used to celebrate all Hindu festivals, such as Holi, Diwali, Basant, etc. A study of different Hindi poems of Nadirat-e-Shahi suggests that various Muslim and Hindu festivals were celebrated with equal enthusiasm and on all such occasions music had a special role. The King used to participate in such celebrations. Following are some examples of these poems :

Diwali

(हमीर, बंधा तिताला)

ए री माई आज अति ही आनन्द सों सब गुनी करें पूरी सुहाली ।
शाहे आलम पिया के मन्दिर भई रोशनी जगमगात की रात दिवाली ॥

(अड़ाना-चौताला)

आज दीवाली आई शुभ शाहे आलम घर है आनन्द बधाई ।
नर नारी गावत बजावत - दीनी मुबारकी सब मिल धाई ॥

Id

(तोड़ी-इकताला)

ए री माई क्या नीको भई आज यह नवेदे रोज़े सईद ।
'शाहे आलम' तुमको मुबारक होवे ईद बक़रीद ॥

(तोड़ी-चौताला)

रब रखे तुम्हारो तख्त ताज नित कायम यही सबके मन रे
हज़ारों साल सुख सम्पत सूँ रहे पीतम प्यारे तिहारो तन रे
आज के रोज़ सभी मिल-मिल जावें और वार दई सब धन रे
तुमको यह ईद मुबारक होवे शाहे आलम पिया प्यारे बन रे

Holi

(सोरठ, होरी)

होरी खेलन आई सबै मिल अपने कन्त सूँ सावरी गोरी
हाथ भरी पिचकारी है रंग की, अबीर गुलाल लिए भर झोरी
दफ़मिरदंग बजावत गावत केसर रंग में है सब बोरी
खेलत फाग में घात सूँ प्यारे कन्हैया ने मोरी बांह मरोरी

Govardhan Puja

(भूपाली बंधातिताला)

गोधन पूजन बन-बन आई सब ही ब्रिज की नारी
गावत राग हुतास भरे अत ही आनन्द सूं नाचत गोप कुमारी

Shab-e-Baraat

(अड़ाना-चौताला)

देखत बाग बहार जहाँ, शाहे आलम, फूली सुहाई लता रे
गावत राग कनचन बाजत बीन, रबाब, तंबूर, अलि तारे
होत आनंद सूँ नौबत बाढ़ी गुन्जत कन्जर जोर नारे
आज शबरात की रात है आली री टूट रहे चहुं ओर सितारे

Some of the songs of this book describe the names of Raags within them, as illustrated by the examples given below :

(गौड़-आड़ा चौताला)

आयो नीको शुभ दिन आज चारंशबे को सुख सूँ सैर कीजे बाग की
शाहे आलम बादशाह ऐश इशरत करो तुम सुनो बातें गौड़ राग की

(अड़ाना-इकताला)

समधन से समधी यूँ बोला मुझे अड़ाना आवे
समधन बोली मुझे चटाचट ताल सवारी भावे

In soms of the songs, the names of the instruments have also been incorporated, from which we can get a clue to the important instruments used at that time.

Following is an illustration of such songs :

(अड़ाना-इकताला)

वीन रबाब तम्बूरा सितार कानून दमामे सारिंगी मुहचंग
झांझ मंजीरा और ढोलकी दाइरा बांसरी करह और ही चंग
खटकरी और कटतार लिए सुरनाई भली करनाई अबपंग
गाय गुनी शाह आलम को सब देत मुबारकी बजाये मिरदंग

In some of the songs, there is a reference to the name of relatives of Shah-Alam. For instance, in the following songs there is a reference to his son Akbar Shah and [his daughter Begum Jaan :

(एमन-चौताला)

गावत मंगलचार गुनी मिल नाच लखें धन बारि दियो है
दादी फूफी खुशहाल फिरें मन अंग समात न फूल गयो है
तारे दिखाए के लेत बलाएं सो मन्दिर बीच विनोद नयो है
अकबर शाह के नन्द भयो सबके घर बीच अनंद भयो है ।

(भूपाली-इकताला)

बेगम जान के पुत्र भयो, ताकी छठी सब देत बधाई
आये सबे तिय चाय बढ़ाय के ले ले बलायें करें मनभाई

Although there is a reference of the Raag and Taal in which the songs were composed, the particular style and form is not indicated anywhere. This is a major deficiency of this work.

There are nine chapters in Nadirat-e-Shahi, and the total number of songs is 606. Out of these, there are 58 Ghazals in Urdu and Persian, 26 Seethne (the songs to be sung on the occasions of marriage), 300 Dohrey and Kavitt, 125 Mubarak Jashne, 20 Mehndis on Gaus Azam, 60 Horis and 16 Taranas.

1. Risala-e-Zikr-e-Mughannian-e-Hindustan

This manuscript is placed in the Khuda Bakhsh Library at Patna. It was written in A.D. 1734-35 by Inayat Khan 'Rasikh'. This book contains the biographies of fifteen well-known musicians of medieval period of Hindustan. The author has described the purpose of writing this book in the following words :

"India has had many great musicians who had no parallel in the world. Such musicians are known as Nayaks. However, very little has been written about such musicians. I have always wondered why authors write the biographies of poets and not of the musicians. After a great deal of thought I came to the conclusion that the great musicians devoted most of their time to the practice and performance, and they did not give any importance to reading and writing about this art. Consequently, their art disappeared with them. However, about a few famous artistes there are brief descriptions regarding their interesting facets of life in some history books on the basis of which I have compiled these biographies. I have consulted the following works to write this book : (1) Shahjahan Nama (2) Mirat-e-Sikandari"[1]

This manuscript was published for the Department of Arabic and Persian by Syed Ali Haider, Professor, Arabic and Persian Research Institute, Patna. The editor of the book states that since the material of this book has been taken from Shahjahan Nama and Mirat-e-Sikandari, which are the books of history, therefore, Risala-e-Zikr-e-Mughannian-e-Hindustan may also be considered as a work of historical nature. The editor has given following details of Inayat Khan, the writer of this book :

Inayat Khan was a resident of Panipat and he belonged to Herat in Afghanistan. His great grandfather came to India during Ghiasuddeen Balban's time (1266-1285 A.D.). It is estimated that he was born in the A.H. 1114. (A.D. 1702).[2] He had five other brothers whose names were :

1. Inayat Khan Rasikh : Risala-e-Zikr-e-Mughannian-e-Hindustan ; edited by S.A. Haider ; p. 5.
2. Inayat Nama : Patna University.

(1) Hidayatullah (2) Fakhir Khan (3) Shakir Khan (4) Mohammad Ibrahim (5) Nasirudden Khan.

Inayat Khan wrote two more books :

(1) **Inayat Nama**—This manuscript is available in Bankipur, Patna, Library. It describes the old and contemporary poets. It contains fourteen chapters and hundred sections.

Falha-e-Hafiz Sheerazi—This is about the Faal of Hafiz Sheerazi. In this book there is a mention of Jahangir Badshah, who was at that time known as Sultan Saleem.

(2) Risala-e-Zikr-e-Mughannian-e-Hindustan is written on green coloured paper which has been damaged by moths, therefore, it is difficult to read this manuscript. The date of writing this copy is not indicated on the manuscript. It has been signed by Khaleefa Mohammed Wasiuddeen. On first page there is a stamp of Abdul Hakim Qadri which indicates 1899 A.D. as the year of its writing.[1] It contains thirty pages. Following are the names of fitfeen musicians described in the book : (1) Nayak Baiju (2) Nayak Gopal (3) Amir Khusrau (4) Nayak Bakshoo (5) Tansen (6) Lal Khan (7) Khushhal and Bisram (8) Baba Ramdas Bairagi and Nayak Dhondhu (9) Sultan Hussain Sharqui (10) Baz Bahadur and Rupmati (11) Sheikh Sher Mohammad—Sheikh Kabir (12) Sheikh Moinuddin (13) Zulqarn (14) Budh Singh (15) Niyamat Khan.

In the end of the book Umar Khayyam's following Rubai has been written :

هر نقش قدم را افسری می گوید
هر کهنه خرابه از دری می گوید
دنیا است فسانه پاره ما گفتیم
آن پاره که ماند دیگری می گوید

On the basis of the above description, it may be concluded that Risala-e-Zikr-e-Mughannian-e-Hindustan is a fine historical study of the life and works of some of the great Indian musicians during the medieval period, when there was no tradition of writing such biographies.

2. Parijatak

(Translation of Pt. Ahobal's Sangeet Parijat)

One of the outstanding works written during the period of

1. Risala-e-Zikr-e-Mughannian-e-Hindustan; edited by S.A. Haider. See Introduction by S.A. Haider.

Aurangzeb is the translation of Sangeet Parijat of Pt. Ahobal by Mirza Roshan Zameer. This manuscript is available in Maulana Azad Library at Aligarh. Safdar Ali from Barsat Ka Qasba has been mentioned as the scribe of this copy. It is also available in the Reza Library at Rampur.

Mirza Roshan Zameer was a famous scholar of his time. He had equal command of Arabic, Persian and Hindi languages. He was also a poet in these languages, and once Aurangzeb awarded him a prize of Rupees seven thousand for one of his Rubaiyat.[1] Aurangzeb appointed Mirza Roshan Zameer as the Bakshi and chronicler of Surat in 1665. A.D. The Persian Parijatak is not only a translation of the original work, but is also a commentry on it. After careful study of this book we find that word to word translation of Parijat has not been done, but its contents have been written in the writer's own language. Since Roshan Zameer was himself a scholar of music, his translation is authentic and of a high standard. According to Sher Khan Lodi Roshan Zameer wrote a few more books on music in Arabic, Persian and Hindi, but unfortunately none of them is traceable.[2]

Wherever Zameer differed from Ahobal, he has elaborated his own viewpoints. Where he was not satisfied he has elaborated the point and described it in detail in his own way. In the same way he has left out some unnecessary parts of the original book. For instance, he has eliminated the last part of Parijatak which he felt unnecessary. It appears that he had access to the original Parijat and commentray on it.[3] Parijatak is divided into three Kands (parts) : (1) Geet Kand—It deals with the principles for Geet. (2) Vadya Kand—It is about musical instruments. (3) Nritya Kand—It is concerned with the art of dancing.

3. Kitab-e-Nauras

This book is a collection of fifty nine Dhruvapad songs composed by Sultan Ibrahim Adil Shah II (1580-1627 A.D.). Although the actual title of the book is Kitab-e-Nauras, some scholars have described it as Nauras-Nama. The rationale for

1. Ansari, N.H. : Farsi Adab ba Ahd-e-Aurangzeb; p. 451.
2. Mirat-ul-Khayal; p. 162
3- Ansari, N.H. : Farsi Adab ba-Ahd-e-Aurangzeb ; p. 452.

naming the book Nauras has been given in its introduction in the following words :

"The reason for giving this title is that Indians call it a mixture of nine juices 'Nauras', and if Persians regard it as a new fruit of the tree of excellence and perfection, it is quite appropriate".[1]

The manuscripts of the work are available in Salar Jung Museum, Hyderabad, Prince of Wales Museum, Bombay, Khuda Bakhsh Khan Oriental Public Library, Patna, Reza Library Rampur, and a few more places in South India.

The exact date of completion of this book is not known; it is, however, certain that the book which embodies a collection of songs could not have been composed on one occasion, but roughly it is estimated that this book was completed sometime between 1006-1012 A.H. (1597-1603 A.D.).[2]

Dr. Nazeer Ahmad of Aligarh Muslim University has edited this book and it was published by Bharatiya Kala Kendra in 1956. Dr. Ahmad has given a detailed introduction of the book. He has quoted Mr. B.G. Gyani of the Prince of Wales Museum, Bombay, who wrote an exhaustive article on the book, based on the manuscript of the Prince of Wales Museum, Bombay. According to Mr. Gyani : "Kitab-e-Nauras is a collection of stray songs composed from time to time and the songs were meant to be sung in different melodies of Indian music, and all the pieces are independent of each other, having nothing like a continuous narration on any particular subject. The book fully indicates the author's command over the language and the subject or the theme and his religious tolerance".[3]

Dr. Nazeer Ahmad has given the following description of the book :

At the beginning of each song or Geet the particular Raag or Ragini in which it was to be sung is mentioned. Each song is divided into three scientific stages : the first stage should be regarded as Sthayi (though the term appears in no song), the second is Bain or Antara, and the last stage is Abhog. It is strange that the divisions of none of the songs correspond to

1. Kitab-e-Nauras; edited by Nazeer Ahmad, p. 55.
2. Ibid., p. 58.
3. Ibid. p. 61.

the four scientific stages through which a Dhruvapad song passes. The Sanchari or the third stage is completely absent from the book. It seems to be Sultan's own creation, and it was on this account that Jahangir, while paying a tribute (in his Tuzuk-e-Jahangiri) to Ibrahim Adil Shah's accomplishments in music, especially in the Dhruvapad form, has called him the expounder of this system which should be considered mid-way between Dhruvapad and Khayal.[1] The author was aware of the classification of Raags and Raginis, but he does not strictly follow this classification.

A study of the songs of Nauras familiarizes us with the various musical instruments commonly used in Deccan, during the author's time. Following fourteen musical instruments can be identified from these songs[2]: (1) Tambourine (2) Kamacha (an instrument having four strings, it had bars for the guidance of notes) (3) Rubab (an instrument having four strings, it had no bars and was played with a plectrum) (4) Jantar (a string instrument) (5) Chhang—(a string instrument) (6) Dhulak (7) Daf (8) Khartal (9) Mridang (10) Shehnai (11) Pawa (12) Nai (13) Khalu (14) Upang.

The fiftynine songs given in Kitab-e-Nauras were composed in seventeen Raags. There are also seventeen Dohras on various topics having great poetic beauty which have been interspersed between the songs. But no particular Raag has been indicated for singing the Dohras. Following are the names of seventeen Raags pertaining to the songs of Nauras: Raags with numbers of songs : (1) Bhupali, 2 (2) Ramkri, 2 (3) Bhairav, 6 (4) Hajiz, 1 (5) Maru, 2 (6) Asavari, 2 (7) Desi, 1 (8) Purba, 1 (9) Barari, 1 (10) Todi, 4 (11) Mallar, 5 (12) Gauri, 2 (13) Kalyan, 4 (14) Dhanasri, 2 (15) Kanhra, 19 (16) Kedar, 4 (17) Nauroz, 1.

Most of the songs deal with the Hindu gods and deities, which is an evidence of the Sultan's tolerance of all faiths. We come across various poems in which the author has referred to Airawat, Hanuman, Sita, Rama, Kamdeva, Parvati and many other religious mythological figures of Hindus. For example, following song gives a description of Ganesh and Saraswati :

1. Ibid, p. 68.
2. Ibid., p. 73.

दर मुक़ाम मलार नौरस

गनपति मूरत हस्त मेघ मद बरसत पानी
दन्त दामिनी घंट घोर गोर मंडान भाल बिधु बानी

आभोग

सरसुती पवित्र स्वांति घन जल कैसे जिय जानी
इबराहीम नौरस मगुता निकसत या कारननहिये मानी[1]

Along with the mention of the Hindu gods and deities, we also find his attachment to Muslim saints. For example, he has written a song in praise of Syed Hussain-e-Gesu Daraz, the renowned saint of Gulbarga. In various songs Ibrahim describes some of the domestic and personal incidents. His attachment to his favourite Tambourine, which he named Moti Khan, can be noted in the following song :

दर मुक़ाम मलार नौरस

झनन झनन झन मोती खां की तांत गाजे
ताल मिरदंग भेद सों नवरस बाजे

अन्तरा (बैन)

इस जग में दो कुछ लीजे
इक तम्बूरा इक कामिनी कीजे

आभोग

इबराहीम जब तूँ बूझे
तब बिहिस्त अमृत क्या करूं मूझें[2]

In another song Sultan describes the beauty, intellect, skilfulness, and other virtues of his wife in the following manner :

दर मुक़ाम तोड़ी नवरस

धन्य बीबी चाँद सुलतान मलके जहां
उत्तिम सुन्दर नारी ऐसी कहां

अन्तरा बैन

रोम रोम चातुर सब भेद सम्पूर अति महा गुण
सारय्यां लाज ढक्यां नारय्यां ऐसी तुव कीरत सुन

1. Kitab-e-Nauras; p. 9.
2. Ibid., p. 110

आभोग

अमृत वचन बुधवंत निर्मल मन एक चित्त एक भांव
इबराहीम रीझा पल-पल लोचन पग कर चल मैं आंव[1]

After the study of Nauras, we come to the conclusion that although Kitab-e-Nauras is not a book on the principles of music and its technique, still it is a significant contribution of Ibrahim Adil Shah which provides useful material for understanding the state of art of music in the early part of seventeenth century.

4. Sahas Rasa

Sahas Rasa (Sahasra Rasa) is a collection of one thousand Dhruvapad songs composed by Nayak Bakshoo. This collection was compiled in accordance with the directives of Emperor Shahjahan. Two copies of this manuscript are available in India Office Library, London, and their photostat copies can be obtained from Sangeet Natak Akademi, New Delhi.

The information about Nayak Bakshoo's contributions is available from several sources which have been described below:

According to Shahjahan Numa, Nayak Bakshoo Kalawant was patronised by Raja Man of Gwalior. He has made significant contribution in raising the standard of Hindustani Music. His rendering of Dhruvapad form was of very high order. His incomparable singing outshadowed all his contemporaries. While singing he used to play Pakhawaj also. His style of Alap singing was unique. After the death of Raja Man, his son Vikramajit gave patronage to Bakshoo. When the fort of Gwalior was taken over by Raja Kirat of Kalinjar, Bakshoo went to Kalinjar. Later Sultan Bahadur Gujrati requested Raja Kirat to send Bakshoo over to his court, and with great hesitancy and sorrow Raja Kirat sent Bakshoo, who spent the rest of his life at Sultan Bahadur's court.[2]

Apart from the above mentioned points, it has been stated in Risala-e-Zikr-e-Mughannian-e-Hindustan that Nayak Bakshoo was brought up by Raja Mansingh. His voice was unparalleled in quality. During those days it was a common practice for at least two persons to sing together, but Nayak Bakshoo used to sing alone. His accomplishment in singing

1. Ibid., p. 108.
2. Shahjahan Nama; p. 223.

stood unrievalled for about one hundred and fifty years.[1]

According to Mirat-e-Aftab Numa, Nayak Bakshoo could sing upto a very high pitch and he innovated a few Raags : (1) Bahaduri Todi—A combination of Todi and Deshkar. (2) Nayki Kanhra—A combination of Kanhra and Shyam. (3) Nayki Kalyan—This Raag was composed by bringing some changes in Kalyan.

The author of Mirat-e-Aftab Numa further states that according to some people he used to dress like saints and lived in the courts of aristocrats. But the person so described was named Baksu, and was different from Nayak Bakshoo.[2]

According to Raag Darpan of Faqueerullah, Bakshoo was a contemporary of Raja Man and he had come to a place known as Kurukshetra on the bank of river Ganges to take holy bath. He composed three new Raags, namely : Bahaduri Todi, Nayki Kalyan, and Nayki Kanhra. Raja Man Singh innovated the style of Dhruvapad with the help of Nayak Bakshoo and other Nayaks of his time.[3]

Surprisingly, Nayak Bakshoo and Baiju have been described in similar terms in a number of Persian works, whereas in reality they were two different persons. Among these works, Mirat-e-Sikandari and Sautun-Naqush deserve special mention. In Sautun-Naqush[4] there is no mention of Bakshoo and only Baiju has been described. However, the details given regarding Baiju completely resemble the description of Nayak Bakshoo.[5]

Sahas Rasa has been edited by Dr. Prem Lata Sharma, and it was published by Sangeet Natak Akademi, New Delhi, in 1972. According to the editor, following is a brief description of the book :

"At the outset of this manuscript an introduction of the book is given. A summary of the same is given below :

1. Inayat Khan Rasikh : Risala-e-Zikr-e-Mughannian-e-Hindustan; pp.11-12.
2. Inayat Khan Rasikh : Risala-e-Zikr-e-Mughannian-e-Hindustan; p. 39.
3. Faqueerullah : Raag Darpan ; p. 39.
4. Sautun-Naqush (Sound of Shankh) was published in 1884 from Nawal Kishore Press.
5. Inayat Khan Rasikh : Risala-e-Zikr-e-Mughannian-e-Hindustan.

'Shahjahan developed a great liking for Dhruvapad compositions of Bakshoo. The compositions were endowed with a blending of the beauty of word and meaning, adherence of Shastrik rules and regulations, novelty of thought content, and delicate handling of word and tone. He ordered that a compilation of authentic compositions of Bakshoo may be made. Musicians from far and wide were invited for this purpose and two thousand songs were noted down for their oral tradition. After a process of sifting, one thousand compositions were finally selected for the compilation".[1]

Sahas Rasa contains 1004 song texts which are composed in Dhruvapad style. It is interesting to note that these songs are composed in only four Raags, viz., Bhairav, Malkauns, Hindol and Shree, instead of six Raags—a system which was popular during that period. Following are the names of Raags and Raginis and the number of songs grouped under these Raags : Raags— Bhairav-30, Malkauns-5, Hindol-15, Shree-40. Raginis—Vibhas-15, Deskara-25, Ramkali-20, Gujari-31, Desakha-10, Bilawal-18, Alaiya-5, Suha-25, Sughrai-12, Pancham-10, Gandhar-16, Khat-15, Puriya-12, Gunkali-15, Todi-40, Desi-10, Dhanasri-7, Malshri-20, Jaitsri-15, Asavari-30, Malhar-18, Nata-10, Gaund-20, Madhmad-6, Savant-10, Sarang-30, Gaud Sarang-5, Marwa-30, Purbi-7, Gauri-16, Travana-15, Kamod-21, Bhupali-50, Kalyan-45, Hameer Kalyan-15, Jait Kalyan-10, Eman Kalyan-5, Syam Kalyan-12, Chhayanat-15, Kanhra-102, Adana-35, Shankarabharana-7, Jaijaiwanti-15, Kedar-50. Eman-Kedar-7, Bihagda-7.

Regarding the Raags, Dr. Prem Lata Sharma feels : "It can be safely concluded that Raag-Ragini scheme of Sahas Rasa does not conform to any specific tradition. There is not a single song in the compilation depicting Raag-Dhyana. It can, therefore, be said that the compiler of Sahas Rasa spoke of Raag and Ragini, because of the fashion of the day, without imbibing the spirit of that system".[2]

While discussing the various Talas, the editor mentions that in the Sahas Rasa all the names of Talas, except Jhoomar

1. Sharma, Prem Lata : Synopsis of treatise, Sahas Rasa : Indian Music Journal, Vols. VIII-IX-X.

2. Sharma, Prem Lata : Synopsis of treatise, Sahas Rasa : Indian Music Journal, Vols. VIII-IX-X.

Taal, have been described in our Shastric texts in the category of Desi Talas. The characteristics of all the Talas other than Kamal Mantha Tala have been described in Sangeet Ratnakar, which was written before Bakshoo's time. Kamal Mantha Tala has been mentioned in the Sangeet Raj of Maharana Kumbha. We must keep in mind that we have no evidence to indicate whether all the names of Talas which are mentioned in Sahas Rasa have not changed. It is quite probable that over two hundred years' time these names might have changed. Further we should not forget that this compilation has been done on the basis of spoken words.

The songs of Sahas Rasa are composed in the language of Gwalior, which has close resemblance to Braj Bhasha. At some places a few Persian and Sanskrit words have also been used in it. The language of these compositions is characterized by fluency and sweetness.

In most of the verses, Emperor Shahjahan's name has been mentioned. Another point which deserves attention is that Sahas Rasa gives an idea about Shahjahan's knowledge and understanding of music. The following verses are noteworthy in this context :

1. निखाद हस्ती कहियत सो सुनी तुम गुनी कंठ तान ।
खरज मोर पिक पंचम धैवत हैं वर जान ।
रिखभ बिरखब गंधार अजा मध्यम क्रौंच परमान ।
कली अन्तर कली काकली ते सब ममझत साहजहाँ सुरज्ञान ।।

2. ता पाछें करम सों गिन-गिन अच्छर ।
धरो प्रथम नाद की, अतीत विचार करो गुनी ।।
सरगम पदमन, सुरत बाईस वादी चार ।
इक्कीस मूर्च्छना, तीन ग्राम, ता मध्र गावत गुनी गंधर्प गंधार गुनी ।।
अवडव षाडव सम्पूरन पूरब अपूरब प्रौढ़ विस्तार मग गन रूप
जोई बतावे, साईं जान निपुनी ।
नशट उदिशट संख्या कर दिखावै ताल काल ग्रह की
अंग, कला, मारग, देसी, वाहि जाने चुनी
साहजहाँ परबीन पैं सीखी सुनी ।।

Dr. Prem Lata Sharma, editor of the published Sahas Rasa, has given her own observations in the following words :

"As regards the songs dealing with the enumeration of Shastrik concepts, the following points are notable. :

(1) The repeated mention of Gram-Murchhana, but the total absence of Mela or Thata.

(2) Numerous references to Bharat-Mata and Saptadhyay (Sangeet Ratnakar).

(3) The profuse mention of technical terms like Dhatu-Matu, Bhajana, Sthaya, Marga Nashtoddishta, etc., which are not much in vogue today.

(4) Repeated reference to the Shuddha-Chhayalag Sankeerna categories of Raags and inspite of a few stray references to Raag-Ragini, the absence of a definite viewpoint in this context.

(5) Special importance given to Tana in singing.

(6) In the context of Shuddha-Vikrita Svaras, the mention of twelve Vikrita Svaras according to Sangeet Ratnakar and the total silence about medieval names of Vikrita Svaras like Komala Tivra or their synonyms.

(7) A few small innovations—the number of sixteen Gamakas instead of the fifteen of Sangeet Ratnakar.

(8) Mention of Desi terms which are not found in Sanskrit texts but are in use in Hindustani music even today, e.g., Shuddha-Mudra, Bani, Urapa, Tiripa, Laga-Dana, etc.

"It can be inferred from the above points that the basic concepts of Sangeet Ratnakar had not become incomprehensible at the time of the creation and compilation of these songs (15th to 17th century A.D.) at least in musical circles, as distinct from the temporary musicological texts".[1]

From the foregoing discussions we come to the conclusion that Sahas Rasa is a rich collection of songs, which gives a clear idea of the thought content and style of Dhruvapad during the seventeenth century.

5. Mirat-e-Aftab Numa

This treatise was compiled in the forty-fiifth year of Shah Alam's reign in A.H. 1217, by Abdul Rehman (entitled Shah Nawaz Hashmi Burhani Dehlvi). The reasons for the book's title are : (1) it gives the alphabetical equal of the numerical A.H. 1218, (A.D. 1803-4), the year of finishing of the book; and (2) Aftab was the poetical Takhallus (pseudonym) of Shah

1. Sharma : Sahas Rasa, synopsis of treatise; *Indian Music Journal*, Vols. VIII-IX-X.

Alam. Copies of this manuscript are kept in the India Office Library, London and British Museum Library. One copy of this manuscript is also kept in the Reza Library at Rampur. A photostat copy of this manuscript is available in Sangeet Natak Akademi, New Delhi, but it has only twenty seven folios (54 pages). National Archives too have got a manuscript with the same title with about four hundred pages, while the copy at British Museum has three-hundred and fifty folios. Mirat-e-Aftab Numa is a general book of history and biographies.

Considerable part of this book has been devoted to Hindustani music and musicians. The biographies of musicians are also given in detail. It offers very good potential for research which should be explored further.

6. Khulasat-ul-Aish-Alam Shahi

This work was written during A.H. 1177 (A.D. 1763-64) by Roshan-Uddaula Rustam Jung Zafar Khan. This book is available in many libraries of north India. The author of the book has borrowed and copied material from several other sources. He has consulted Tohfat-ul-Hind extensively and has almost copied its entire chapter on Sangeet.

7. Tashrih-ul-Mousiqi

This is a translation of Bodh Prakash which was written during Tansen's time. The author of this work is Mohammad Akbar Arzani. He was a well-known Hakeem who has written a number of books on medicine. Like Man Kautuhal of which only a translation (Raag Darpan) is available, so also Bodh Prakash is available only in the translated form. This manuscript is available in the Shirani collection of Punjab University at Lahore.[1]

8. Muftah-ul-Sarod

This book was written by Qazi Hasan Bin Khwaja Tahir Bin Khwaja Mohammad. The author of this book was the Qazi of Pargana Antur (Daultabad). He wrote this book in A.D. 1673.

In the Asiatic Society of Calcutta, there is a book entitled Misbah-ul-Saroor, which is an extended and enlarged version of this small booklet.[2] This book contains four chapters describ-

1. Ansari, N.H. : Farsi Adab ba Ahd-e-Aurangzeb; p. 460.
2. Ibid., p. 459.

ing Raag-Raginis and different varieties of musical instruments. The author has stated that in his time there were four authoritative books on music : (1) Sangeet Ratnakar (2) Roop Ratnakar (3) Sangeet Makrand (4) Bharat Sangeet.

The first three were popular in Deccan, while Bharat Sangeet was considered an authoritative and reliable book in northern India.[1]

9. Marfat-Ul-Naghm

The author of this book was Abdul Hassan Qaisar. It was written during 1676 A.D. The music of India and Iran has been discussed in this book. The writer has consulted other contemporary reliable sources for writing this book.[2]

10. Shams-Ul-Aswat

This book is a translation of a Sanskrit or Hindi book entitled 'Sangeet'. It was written in A.D. 1697-98. The name of the translator is given as Ras Baras. The writer has mentioned his father's name Khushhal Khan Kalawant. There are six chapters in this book.[3]

In addition to the above mentioned important works, there are a number of other books on Hindustani Music in Persian and Urdu languages which were written during the eighteenth century and early part of the nineteenth century A.D., and most of them have been published. Following is a short list of such books : 1. Risala-Mousiqi (This book was dedicated to Prince Mohammad Azam. It contains an introduction and thirteen chapters). 2. Tohfatul-Naghmat by Syed Mohammad Ruhulla. 3. Naghmatul-Hind by Mohammad Ashfaq Ali Khan *urf* Nawab Jaani Sahib Rais Bilai 4. Sarmaya-e-Ishrat by Sadiq Ali Khan 5. Qanoon-e-Mousiqi by Sadiq Ali Khan 6. Naghma-e-Dilruba by Jung Baz 7. Naghma-e-Jaan Fiza by Hussain Khan 8. Ghuncha-e-Rag by Mardan Ali Khan of Moradabad 9. Naghma-e-Saadat by Sahebzada Saadat Ali Khan 10. Marifun-Naghmat (4 volumes) by Raja Nawab Ali Akbarpur 11. Madnul-Mousiqi by Karam Imam Khan 12. Hayat-e-Amir Khusrau by Naqi Mohammad Khar

1. Ansari, N.H. Farsi Adab ba-Ahd-e-Aurangzeb; p. 459.
2. Ibid., p. 460.
3. Ibid., p. 460.

13. Ragmala (Persian translation) 14. Sautun-Naqoosh 15. Hazrat Amir Khusrau Ka Ilme-Mousiqi Aur Doosre Maqalat by Rashid Ahmad 16. Taskera-e-Mirat-ul-Khayal by Amir Sher Khan Lodhi 17. Ilm-e-Raag 18. Naghma-e-Sanam 19. Majmaul-Uloom 20. Risala-e-Raag 21. Risala-e-Mousiqi 22. Raag Chaman 23. Hindustan Ki Mousiqi by Abdul Haleem Sharar 24. Hamari Mousiqi (Karachi-Pakistan).

SECTION B

Development of Forms and Styles in Hindustani Music during Seventeenth and Eighteenth Centuries

IN the foregoing chapters various important manuscripts pertaining to the seventeenth and eighteenth centuries have been discussed. It has been noted that most of the writings during this period have given descriptions of the various forms and styles of music which were popular during that period, and there are indications of changes and innovations introduced during that period. The purpose of this section is to examine in detail the forms and styles of music prevalent during the seventeenth and eighteenth centuries, and to identify the significant changes, improvisations, and innovations introduced during that period. For this purpose Dhruvapad, Khyal, Tarana, Thumri, Qawwali and Qaul have been analysed in detail in this Section. The first two chapters have been devoted to Dhruvapad and Khyal, and the various other forms and styles have been briefly examined in the third chapter of this Section on the basis of a study of the literature pertaing to that period.

CHAPTER V

Dhruvapad : Its Origin and Development

THE word Dhruvapad is a combination of two words—Dhruva and Pada. Dhruva means anything which is fixed, diterminate, definite, permanent or immovable, and Pada means the verbal text. Therefore, Dhruvapad is a song in which the Padas or words are well set in a definite structure. Dhruva has been discussed in Natyashastra of Bharata in detail. Dhruvas were the stage songs which were employed to enhance the effect of the different situations occurring in a dramatic performance. In these dramatic songs the Varna, Alankar, Jati and Pani occurred regularly. They were of five classes :

(1) Praveshiki —It was related to entrance
(2) Aksepiki —It was related to diversion
(3) Naiskramiki —It was related to departure
(4) Prasadiki —This was for calming down the audience
(5) Antara —It was related to transition.

A careful study of Dhruva songs of Natyashastra reveals that there is no significant similarity between Dhruvas and Dhruvapad form of singing, because they look different from each other in the structure and application. However, medieval writers have related Dhruvapad with particular type of dances. According to them, Dhruvapad Nritt was a dance form in which Dhruvapad was sung as an accompaniment. For example, Abul Fazl in his Ain-e-Akbari, while describing the women known as Dufzan, has stated :

"Dufzan are chiefly Punjabi women who play on the Duffs and Dhol and sing Dhruvapad and Sohela or nuptial and birthday songs. Formerly they appeared before women but now they exhibit in public".[1]

In the same manner, Shivaji's father Shahji's Sabha Pandit (court priest) Ved has described Dhruvapad Nritt in the following words :

गीयमाने ध्रुवपदे गीते भावमनोहरे
नर्तनं तनुयात् पात्रं कान्ताहास्यादिदृष्टिजम्
नानागतिलसद्भाव मुखरागादिसंयुक्तम
सुकुमारांगविन्यासं दन्तोद्योतितहावकम्
खण्डमानेन रचितं मध्ये मध्ये च कम्पनम्
यत्र नृत्यं भवेदेवं ध्रुपदाख्यं तदा भवेत्
प्रायशो मध्यदेशीयभाषया यत्र धावत:
उद्ग्राहधुवकाभोगास्त्रय एते भवन्ति ते
उदग्राहरहितं केचित्परे त्वाभोगवर्जितम्
उद्ग्राहभोगरहितमन्वर्थमरे जगु: ॥[2]

The essence of the above mentioned quotation is that when Dhruvapad—which is full of feelings—is being sung, the dancer should portray the sentiments and emotions of Nayika, through all the subtle expressions and movements. This dance should be composed in parts, and in between the parts there should be Kampan. Such a dance form is called Dhruvapad. It has three Dhatus (components), namely—Udgrah, Dhruvak and Abhog. It is written in Madhya Deshi language. Some people narrate it without Udgrah and Abhog. In other words, they call it only Dhruvak, which is conveying the same meaning as Dhruvapad. This leads to the conclusion that in the earlier days Dhruvapad was a song which was a part of a particular type of dance. It may be noted that dance was an important part of Natya, according to Natyashastra. Even if we take note of the above mentioned points, it is very difficult to relate the Dhruvapad with Dhruva songs of Natyashastra.

According to most of the writers during the medieval period, Dhruvapad form was originated by Raja Mansingh of Gwalior (1486-1518 A.D). The historian Abul-Fazl, in his

1. Gladwin, Francis : Ain-e-Akbari (translated), p. 734.
2. Anandpal Singh, Sumitra : Dhruvapad Ke Sambandh Mein Bhatkhande Ji Ke Vichar; *Sangeet*, May, 1966.

Ain-e-Akbari has stated that Raja Mansingh 1anwar, the ruler of Gwalior, with the assistance of Nayak Bakshoo, Macchu, and Bhannu, who were the most distinguished musicians of their time, introduced a popular style of melody which was approved even by the most refined taste.[1]

The author of Tohfat-ul-Hind has given the description of this styl ; in the following words :

"A poetic composition which is divided into four parts, and each part of which has a specific name, is known as Dhruvapad. It is said that Raja Mansingh was the innovator of th:s·type of song, but the truth is known only to the God almighty"[2].

According to Faqueerullah, the author of Raag Darpan :

"Dhruvapad is a form composed by Raja Man of Gwalior. He composed this style with the help of Nayak Bakshoo, Bhannoo, Mahmood Lohang and Karna".[3]

دیسی تصانیفِ دھرپد، زادهٔ طبع مان گوالیاری است
چنانچه بالا مذکور شد از چهار مصرع انتظام پاید. در وجمیع سها
بندند. بدستیاری نایک بھنو و بخشو و محمود لوہنگ و کرن.
این قسم چیزی عام خاص پسند بر دی کار آورد که همه جنس
تصانیف ذرجنب آن چیزی نماند. چنانچه دلیل برین
سخن دو دارم. اول آنکه ازان باز که دھرپد شد راگ و
تصانیف مارگ ازیا درافتاد مگر چند راگ که در آن
فتوری راه نیافته مردم سو دیسی بزبان دیسوالی
خوانند چنانچه بالا مذکور شد. دوم اینکه دھرپد
همه چیز را با خود دارد آنچه در جمیع تصانیف مارگ
و دیسی باشد، از همه اندک برگرفته، این قسم
عجوبه به رونی کار آورد.

1. Swami Prajnanand : Historical Study of Indian Music ; p. 164.
2. See Tohfat-ul-Hind, Edited by N.H. Ansari.
3. Raag Darpan, p. 39, of the manuscript.

Similarly, many western writers have expressed their views regarding the innovator of this style, and they also believed that this sort of composition has its origin from the time of Raja Mansingh of Gwalior. They have considered him as the father of Dhruvapad singers. The names of these scholars are: Captain Willard, Sir William Jones, N. Augustus, Sir Ousley and Dr. Griffiths.

But we should not forget that all these statements are based on merely legends, and oral statements of various people. Thus, it is impossible to prove this point historically.

Another viewpoint which deserves consideration is that a sophisticated and complex style of music as Dhruvapad could not have been the innovation of a single person, and it must have evolved as a result of the convergence of the talents of many musicians over a long period of time. But, at the same time, there can be no difference of opinion on the view that Mansingh extended his full support and patronage to this style, and took keen interest in the revival and development of this style. This point is supported by the fact that all the musicians in the court of Mansingh, as described in the various books, were renowned Nayaks and most of them were accomplished Dhruvapad performers, and their Dhruvapad compositions remained popular for the next three centuries.

After deep study of our ancient Shastric texts, it can be proved that Dhruvapad evolved from the earlier forms of music which existed in our ancient musical system. On this subject Pt. Ratanjankar is of the opinion that Dhruvapad seems to be related to the tradition of religious hymns which were sung in the ancient temples. In the famous Vaishnavite temples of Nathdwara, Vishnupur, Dwarika, Jagannathpuri, Mathura, Vrindavan, etc., singing and playing instruments along with dancing was performed at the sunrise, sunset and during the night. This tradition survives at some temples even today. These religious songs are accompanied by Mridang. These songs were called Kirtans, which were sung in praise of God. The Sanskrit Prabandhas given in our ancient classical writings are more or less similar to these Kirtans. The Gita Govinda of Jaidev is also a collection of such Prabandhas. Sanskrit was beginning to be replace by Desi, Prakrit languages, such as Brij Bhasha, Purvi, Maithili Bengali, Marathi etc., around the ninth century onwards. Thus, Sanskrit religious songs were being substituted by the songs composed in Desi and Prakrit languages. In this proces the famous poets of Bhakti period, such as Chaitanya Mahaprabhu, Chandidas, Vidyapati, Baiju Bawra, Swami Haridas, etc., composed innumerable religious songs of this kind which were sung in the temples. These songs were well composed and provided scope for Alap and Layakari. Based on the structure of these songs, the court singers developed songs of new Dhruvapad styles in which there was greater stress on artistic and aesthetic aspects. Since the purpose of Dhruvapad sung in temples was to adore god and achieve salvation of the soul, therefore, the intensity of feelings and devotion was of central importance in this style. On the other hand, the Dhruvapad of the court was Laukik (worldly) in which greater importance was attached to artistic variations, ingenuity and skill.[1]

From the above discussion it is evident that Dhruvapad is not an entirely new innovation, and it has evolved from the earlier traditional forms, particularly Parbandhas. The term Prabandha has been described elaborately in our ancient texts. Pt. Sarangdev has dealt with this in grreat detail in his Sangt Ratnakar. He has devoted a whole chapter to Prabandha in his book. He has given the following description of Prabandha :

यत्तु वाग्गेयकारेण रचितं लक्षणान्वितम्
देशी रागादिषु प्रोक्तं तदगानं जनरंजनम्
तत्र गान्धर्व मुक्तं प्रागधुना गानमुच्यते
निबद्धमनिबद्धं तद् द्वेधा निगदितं बुधै:
बद्धं धातुभिरंगैश्च निबद्धमभिधीयते
आलप्तिर्बन्धहीनत्वादनिबद्धमितीरिता
सा चास्माभि: पुरा प्रोक्ता निबंद्ध त्वधुनोच्यते
संज्ञात्रयं निबद्धस्य प्रबन्धो वस्तु रूपकम्
प्रबन्धावयो धातु: स चतुर्था निरूपित:
उद्ग्राह प्रथमस्तत्र ततो मेलापक ध्रुवौ
आभोगश्चेति तेषां च क्रमातलक्ष्माभिदमहे
उदग्राह: प्रथमो भागस्ततो येलापक: स्मृत:

1. Ratanjankar, Krishna Narayan : Dhruvapad Gayaki Ki Samasyaen.

A summarized version of the above definition is given below :

In Sangeet, Ganam is composed and characterized by certain qualities. It is composed in Desi Raags. Its purpose or objective is to give aesthetic pleasure. It is of two varieties—(1) Anibaddham (2) Nibaddham. Anibaddha Gaan is Raag Alapti which is not associated with a composed piece. Nibaddham is well-knit or well-bound by means of its Dhatus and Angas. There are three names of Nibaddham :

(1) Prabandha (2) Vastu (3) Rupak

In this way Prabandha is a variety of Gaan, which is bound up in a systematic way by its four Dhatus (constituent parts) namely, Udgrah, Melapak, Dhruva, Antara and Abhog, and six Angas (limbs) namely Svara, Virud, Pad, Tenak, Pata and Tala. A fifth Dhatu is also described which is Antara. This is occasionally present in certain varieties of Praban has which is called Salag Suda Prabandha. This is sung in between Dhruva and Abhog.

Pt. Sarangdev further states that :

स द्विधातुस्त्रिधातुश्च चतुर्धातुरिति त्रिधा

According to practice prevalent during those days Prabandha consisted of two, three or four Dhatus. It was not necessary that all the varieties of Prabandha should have four Dhatus. When there were only two Dhatus present, it was called Dwidhatu, if three Dhatus were present it was known as Tridhatu and when four Dhatus were present then it was called Chaturdhatu Prabandha. But Dhruva was the only Dhatu which was always present in every composition and it was always repeated several times after completing each part of the Prabandha.

The Angas have been considered as the inner elements of Prabandha. Pt. Sarangdev has given the following descriptions of the Angas of Prabandha :

स्वराभिव्यक्तिसंयुक्ताः स्वरशब्देन कीर्तिताः
विरूदं गुणनाम स्यात्त तोऽन्यद्वाचकं पदम्
तेनेतिशब्दस्तेनः स्यान्मंगलार्थप्रकाशकः
ओं तत्सदिति निर्देशात्तत्वमस्यादिवाक्यतः
तदिति ब्रह्म तेनायं ब्रह्मणा मंगलात्मा

लक्षितस्तेन तेनेति पाटो वाद्याक्षरोत्करः
तालस्तालप्रकरणे सप्रपंचौ निरूप्यते ।

Obviously, Svara is the most fundamental Anga of Prabandha. Virudam means Gunnam or epithets and qualities of great personalities, gods and goddesses. In Virud the qualities of heroes, kings or deities are described. The verbal text is called Pad. Tenak was used for expressing the auspicious and uplifting prepositions which has also been described as Mangalarth Prakashak in our Shastrik texts. For example.

तेन इदं ततं तत् सद् इति

Paat is a group of syllables produced out of musical instruments. In our Shastras the word Vak-Karanya is often used which means to establish similarity between these syllables produced on instruments, with the human voice. This syllabic interpretation of the different sounds produced on different instruments is called Paat. Taal is an essential element of Prabandha. Because Prabandha is basically Nibaddha Gaan which cannot be conceived without Taal.

Depending on the number of Angas present in Prabandha, the following five varieties have been described :

(1) Medini or Shruti — It consists of six Angas
(2) Anandini or Niti — It consists of five Angas
(3) Dipni or Sena — It consists of four Angas
(4) Bhavni or Kavita — It consists of three Angas
(5) Taravali or Champu—It consists of two Angas.

The foregoing description reveals that most of characteristics of Prabandha, described in Sangeet Ratnakar, are comparable to the characteristics of Dhruvapad. Dhruvapad can also be divided into different Dhatus or parts. Its four parts—Sthayi, Antara, Sanchari and Abhog—are often sung in Dhruvapad even today. In some of these compositions one or two parts are missing. Such Dhruvapads can be compared with the Tridhatu and Dwidhatu Prabandhas. Further, it is noteworthy that some of the Dhruvapads pertaining to the medieval period have been discovered which contained only three Dhatus or parts. Kitab-e-Nauras contains several such Dhruvapads. Following is one such example :

दर मुक़ाम देसी नौरस
एक नार देखिया खड़ी सामनी
पुनिम रात की मकर चांदनी
या झमके मेघ रुत सौदामिनी
(बैन) अन्तरा
बहु रूप खेले खेल कामिनी
हो ना जानू तुर्किनी बरहामनी
आपें नर रूप आपे रूप सुहागनी
दस रूप ईश्वर की त्याई निशानी
आभोग
चितारी चितर तसके होये मानी
ज्यों मौज पर मौज आवे पानी
बोले बां तां शीरीं जुबानी
इबराहीम मिलतें चरन धरो पेशानी[1]

Similarly, there are some Dhruvapads of this book which contain as many as five parts. For example

दर मुक़ाम तोड़ी नौरस
संघाती संघात सब सहेलियां संग
करें पीरत केरयां बाजियां झोंट धरनी जंग
बैन (अन्तरा)
होयां हो लट पट सट बिट रंग तरंग
जे देखे भूले मन नव रतन नारी अंग
बैन (अन्तरा)
कदम कस्तूरी केसरी कुसुम रंग
ढोलतियां झूमतियां मद शराब भंग
बैन (अन्तरा)
उत्तिम बहु गुन गावें नवरस आहंग
तम्बूरा रबाव जंतर कमाच चंग
ढोलक डफ हुडुग ताल मिरदंग
शनाई पावा नम ख़ालू उमंग
आभोग
इबराहीम बसन्त खेलें समुद्र गंग
भानू बसन्त विनती करे अरुन रंग भंग[2]

1. Ahmad, Nazeer : Kitab-e-Nauras, p. 105.
2. Ibid.,

An important point worthy of note is that in Ghunyat-ul-Munya, for the middle part of composition the term Dhruvapad has been used instead of Dhruva. While describing Sarood (Gaan) the author says : "When a Gan is sung according to certain well defined rules and patterns, it is called Anibaddha, and when the Gaan is sung according to certain rules and is bound by its different parts it is called Nibaddha. On the other hand, when Anibaddha and Nibaddha are combined it is called Mishra Gaan. There are three varieties of Mishra Gaan : (1) Rupak (2) Prabandha (3) Vastu.

Rupak is based on four parts. Ugah (Udgrah)—This is the first part. Gaan begins through this part. Dhruvapad—This is the central part of the Gaan and is repeated several times. Abhog—This is the last part of the song, and this part is dovoted to the adoration of the person who has arranged the performance. Melavah (Melapak)—Through this part all the three former parts are combined. Likewise, in a song called Jhoomra the central part has also been termed as Dhruvapad.[1]

The above mentioned account of Dhruvapad as central part of Rupak and Jhoomra raises some curiosity about the original form of Dhruvapad. It is possible that Dhruvapad of today, which is an independent musical form in itself, might have been earlier a part of some of the forms as indicated above.

Bhavbhatta has given the following definition in his Anoop Sangeet Ratnakar :

गीर्वाणमध्यदेशीयभाषा साहित्यराजितम्
द्विचतुर्वाक्यसम्पन्नं नरनारी कथाश्रयम्
श्रृंगाररसभावाद्यं रागालापदात्मकम्
पादांतानुप्रासयुक्तं पादानयुगकं च वा
प्रतिपादं यत्र बद्धमेवं पादचतुष्टयम
उदग्राह ध्रुवकाभोगांतरं ध्रुवपदं स्मृतं

According to the above definition, Dhruvapad is a Pad which is composed in the language of Madhya Pradesh, that is Gwaliori, consisting of two or four Tuks (metres), narrating the theme of love dominated by Sringar Ras, and the essence

1. Ghunyat-ul-Munya, edited by Shahab Sarmadee, p. 33-38.

of which is infused with Raag and Alap. The endings of these Padas, and sometimes in between the endings, is artfully decorated with alliterations. It has four parts, namely, Udgrah, Dhruva, Abhog and Antara.

In the definition of Bhavbhatta, the different parts of Dhruvapad have been given the same name as in Prabandha. The only difference is the absence of Melapak. At some places a part named Manjha (the middle part) is also in practice which may possibly be the substitute of Melapak.

In the same way, out of six Angas, three Angas, Svara, Pad and Taal are always present in Dhruvapad. Similarly, Viruda Tenak and Paat can also be used. Pat is already incorporated in Trivat form of singing which is akin to Dhruvapad. The alap (Nom-Tom), which initiates Dhruvapad and is an essential part of it can also be described as a modified version of Tenak.

A close study of the books written during the later medieval period clearly brings to light the transformation of Prabandha into Dhruvapad. Such a transformation came about through gradual decline in the use of Prabandha and some changes in structure and form of Prabandha. Some Dhatus of Prabandha were given a new terminology and some changes were introduced in the verbal texts also which led to the emergence of Dhruvapad style of music. This analysis is brought forth most explicitly in Usulun-Naghmat-e-Asifi, which should be considered an authoritative source for proving this point.

While describing Dhruvapad the author of Usulun-Naghmat-e-Asifi states :

"The forms of music like Dhruvapad have evolved from Geet. Dhruvapad is the essence of Geet, and is composed in Desi Bhasha. It is of five types : (1) Dhruvapad containing five verses (2) Dhruvapad containing four verses (3) Dhruvapad containing three verses (4) Dhruvapad containing two verses (5) Dhruvapad containing one verse.

Each verse has a different title and shape. These parts are also called Dhatus and their names are :

"(1) Udgrah (2) Dhruva (3) Melapak (4) Antara, and, (5) Abhog.

"Udgrah begins with the first note and generally people call it Sthayi. Dhruva refers to an object which is stable and stationary. The other verses keep revolving around Dhruva".

Further the author states : "In my period Dhruvapad is based on four verses or Dhatus :

"**First Verse** : It begins with first note and it is permissible to start with the second note also.

"**Second Verse** : It begins with the third note.

"**Third Verse** : It begins with the fourth note. Occasionally keeping in view Vadi-Samvadi notes, it also begins with the third note.

"**Fourth Verse** : It starts from the sixth and seventh note and may also be started by Teep or eighth note".[1]

The above definitions given in Usulun-Naghmat-e-Asifi abundantly support the conclusion that Dhruvapad adopted the main principles of Prabandha, but with some changes according to prevalent musical atmosphere.

Whereas the beginning of Dhruvapad is believed to be around thirteenth and fourteenth centuries A.D., it seems to have reached its zenith and highest popularity during the sixteenth, seventeenth and eighteenth centuries A.D. According to the description given in Ain-e-Akbari and Raag Darpan, most of the renowned musicians of that time were Dhruvapad singers. Kitab-e-Nauras and Sahas Rasa written during this period are collections of thousands of Dhruvapads. It has been stated in Sahas Rasa that Shahjahan was a great admirer of Dhruvapad compositions of Bakshoo and, therefore, Sahas-Rasa was written under his directions. The popularity of Dhruvapad as far as Deccan is evident from Kitab-e-Nauras, which is a collection of Dhruvapads of high standards in language and compositions, written by Ibrahim Adil Shah, the ruler of Bijapur.

The importance and glory of this form is also manifest in Akbar's period as expressed by the most famous musician Tansen in his own words as given below. In this Dhruvapad, which is Tansen's own composition, he has compared Dhruvapad to a beautiful concealed gem :

.1 Ghulam Reza : Usulun-Naghmat-e-Asifi; pp. 131-132.

नाद नगर बसायौ, सुरपति महल छायौ
उनचास कुटतान अक्षर विश्राम पायौ
गीत छन्द तत वितत घन शिखर कंचन ताल
काल कै किवाड़ अलाप तालो हीरा पैठायौ
पाट नग लगै, खरज जंजीर त्रैवट कुंजी
तामैं ध्रुवपद सौ नग छिपायौ
आरोही अवरोही अस्थाई संचारी ज़बार
अरब खरब औ कठोर मन मिलाप लायौ
जौहरी मियां तानसेन गाहक जलालदीन
जिन चाको मिल कीन्यौ अकबर पारखी गायो

Even during Aurangzeb's time Dhruvapad was popular to the same degree of admiration, as is evident from the following Dhruvapad song which has been compossed in praise of the emperor :

आयो आयो रे महाबलि आलमगीर
जाकी धाक देखे कोऊ धरे न धीर
अनवली तपवली आलीजंग और तेऊ भाटल गंभीर
दक्षिन दलमले विकट गढ़ हलहले
जाको तो धुआई फिरैं दरियातीर
चकतावंश सुलितान औरंग्ज़ेब
साहिनी में साहि औलिया जिन्दापीर

Following is another Dhruvapad song in praise of Jahangir Saani :

देव सुर सुखी रहौ जों लौं गंगा जमुना दरियों पानी
तुमरी रहत जोत सवाई साहब कुरां जहांगीर सानी

We shall now examine the well known books and manuscripts which give an explicit account of Dhruvapad during the seventeenth and eighteenth centuries. Among the various manuscripts examined it was noted that Raag Darpan gives the most detailed description of the popularity of this style in the following words :

"After the innovation of Dhruvapad form, the Prabandha style of singing no more remained in vogue. This form of singing was so widely accepted and practised by the most renowned as well as the common musicians that all other forms of singing disappeared. There are two reasons for this change:

"(1) At the time when Dhruvapad was taking roots, the Margi forms of music were losing popularity and Desvali (Desi) forms of music were being appreciated increasingly. Thus Dhruvapad absorbed the characteristics of both Margi and Desi styles of singing.

"(2) Raja Mansingh had assembled together the most renowned musicians two hundred years ago, who had pooled together their vast and rich musical talents to develop the novel musical form of Dhruvapad in which they assimilated the best features of Margi and Desi Sangeet. The language of this new form incorporated the language of both styles. It would be impossible to create a musical form like Dhruvapad today, even if the same resources and musical talents which were accessible to Raja Mansingh could be utilized for this purpose".[1]

In the same way the writer of Tohfat-ul-Hind has described the popularity of this style in the following words :

"Now I shall describe the Geets which are prevalent and popular at the present time. Among them the first and foremost is Dhruvapad. It consists of four Tuks (parts) and each Tuk is called by different names. These are : (1) Sthal or Sthayi or Peedhabandh (2) Antara (3) Bhog (4) Abhog.

"Phool Bandh—It refers to those Dhruvapads which are named after certain flowers, such as Champa and Chameli. Except for the mention of such flowers there is no other change in the structure.

"Jugal Bandh—When two musicians sing together two different Dhruvapads composed in the same Taal, it is known as Jugal Bandh. Inspite of different compositions being sung together, the musicians have no difficulty in such performance and the two Dhruvapads appear like a single harmonious melody".

In Usulun-Naghmat-e-Asifi, as has been explained earlier, Dhruvapad has been described in much greater detail as compared to other styles of music. According to the author of this book, this style was most widely liked and appreciated by the musicians of his time.

The foregoing detailed study and analysis of Dhruvapad leads to the conclusion that this form of singing has evolved during the last eight centuries, and has gone through several

1. Faqueerullah : Raag Darpan ; pp. 38-39.

variations, blends and refinements. It can be heard even today in its enriched and varied form after passing through all shades of influences during the past centuries, and yet it is the only form which retains its pristine beauty, classic form, and artistic structure. During its long life, the most significant and glorious period of its populaity and enrichment was the span of the seventeenth and eighteenth centuries A.D.

CHAPTER VI

Khayal : Its Origin and Development

KHAYAL is the most popular form of singing and it has a unique place in the present Hindustani Musical System. The word Khayal is described in the Arabic and Persian dictionaries as dream, vision, a day-dream, fancy, imagination, thought, meditation, idea, reflection, apparition and impression. The term Khayal is often used to convey the same meaning as the word Dhyan (meditation) in Hindi. But in the field of music this word refers to a specific form of music. In other words, Khayal is the imaginative and thoughtful verse, which is full of feelings and fancy.

In Rajasthan some particular paintings depicting the incidents of historical events are also called Khayal. Some Lavni (a folk music) singers describe in their songs the historical stories and play Chhang (an instrument) for the accompaniment, and they call these songs Khayal.[1]

Sufis like Shah Burhanuddin (later half of sixteenth century A.D.) composed songs describing the anguish or pain of love and called them Khayal.[2] In Sufism the mystic songs which were composed as Ghazals praising Peers (saint) and prophets were also described as Khayal. In this way Ghazal, Qawwali and Khayal belong to the same category of music. These Khayal singers called it Banda or Langra Dhruvapad. In other words, we can say that Khayal singers gave an answer to the Dhruvapad.[3]

1. Acharya Brahaspati : 'Musalman, Ghazal, Qawwali Aur Khayal' ; Sangeet, Jan-Feb., 1976, p. 61.
2. Acharya Brahaspati : Musalman Aur Bhartiya Sangit, Raj Kamal Prakashan, Delhi, 1974, p. 112.
3. Acharya Brahaspati, 'Muaslman, Ghazal, Qawwali Aur Khayal'; Sangeet, Jan-Feb., 1976.

In northern India, different varieties of drama and dance dominated by musical compositions are found. According to some scholars the word Khayal has been derived from the Hindi word Khel and in due course this word was changed and used as Khayal in local languages.[1] Following are few examples.[2]

1. कंत बीस लोचन विलोकिये कुमंत फल
   खयाल लाई लंका कवि राँड की सी झोंपरी
   (तुलसी कवितावली)
2. कूदि पड़े चढ़ि कदम तैं तुम खेलत यह खयाल
   (सूरदास—सूरसागर)
3. सुनहु सूर वह करनि कहनि यह ऐसे प्रभु के खयाल
   (सूरदास—सूरसागर)
4. चकृत नर नारि करत खयाला
   (सूरदास—सूरसागर)

Following is another example of song in which the word Khel has been used as Khayal :

धमार-राग सिन्दूरा (आगरा घराना)
लाल तुम नये नये खयाल खेलन लागे
कैसे बचेंगे बृज बाल

A special variety of musical poems which are recited by the Sufi saints in southern India is also known as Khayal. The nature of these songs is mystic.[3]

Faqueerullah in his Raag Darpan has mentioned about a special type of musical instrument named Khayal during the time of Shahjahan. This was invented by Sheikh Bahauddin.[4]

The Origin of Khayal

There is a great deal of controversy among the scholars of Indian music about the origin of this style. Different views have been expressed in this connection and it is very difficult to come to a definite conclusion, since these authors do not give any trustworthy, historical evidence in support of their opinion. Following are the two names which are often asso-

1. Shukla, S : 'Khayal Ek Punaravlokan', Sangeet, Jan-Feb., 1976.
2. Ibid., p. 17.
3. Acharya Brahaspati : Musalman Aur Bhartiya Sangeet ; p. 14.
4. Faqueerullah : Raag Darpan ; p. 19.

ciated with the Khayal style by various musicologists : (1) Hazrat Amir Khusrau (2) Sultan Hussain Shah Sharqui.

(1) Hazrat Amir Khusrau

Hazrat Amir Khusrau is often called the innovator of Khayal style. He is considered as a profound genius and a great musician of the thirteenth century. Following is a brief sketch of his life, which would throw light on the kinds of influences on him and his contribution to Hindustani music.

Amir Khusrau was born in the year 1253 A. D. at Patiali. His father, Amir Saifuddin Mohammad, belonged to the tribe Lachin Balkh Hazara. In India he settled down at Patiali, a small town in the district of Etah in U. P., and entered the service of Shamsuddin Iltutmish, the slave king of India.[1]

From his childhood Khusrau showed signs of a literary bent of mind. Unfortunately, his father died when Khusrau was only nine years old.[2] Khusrau spent most of his time in studying poetry and fine arts. He himself describes at one place in his Diwan, Tohfat-us-Singar : "My parents used to send me to the maktab (school) for study, but I repeated only rhymes and my learned teachers tried to teach me calligraphy, while I composed verses about the silken gown on fair faces, As a consequence, I began to compose verses and Ghazals that roused the admiration and wonder of my elders."[3]

Khusrau grew amidst luxury and ease, and passed his youthful days in the society of great men. He listened eagerly to the learned discourses of the scholars, artistic recitals of poets, and the melodious songs of musicians. It was probably in these early days, in the magnificent assemblies convened by Imad-ul-Mulk, that Amir Khusrau imbibed a love for music, a science in which he later acquired great proficiency. [4]

Amir Khusrau enjoyed the patronage of five successive kings, and each of them was a great patron of literature and fine arts. Musical sittings were held regularly in the court of Ghiasuddin (A. D. 1265-1287). His son Mahmood invited Sheikh Qadwa, son of Sheikh Bahauddin Zakaria, and other Sufis of his time, and musical conferences were held in which Ara-

1. Mirza Waheed : The Life and Works of Amir Khusrau; Idarah-i-Adabiya-e-Delli, 1935, p. 15.
2. Ustad Chand Khan : Mousiqui Hazrat Amir Khusrau; p. 197.
3. Mirza, Waheed : The Life and Works of Amir Khusrau; p. 20.
4. Mirza, Waheed ; The Life and Works of Amir Khusrau, p. 20.

bic Ghazals were sung.[1] The Prince was so much impressed by Khursrau's talent that he often used to invite Khusrau and presented him precious gifts. In A.D. 1274, when Punjab was attacked by Mughals, prince Mahmood took Amir Khusrau to the battle field along with him[2].

In the court of Jalaluddin Khilji the Ghazals of Khusrau were regularly recited by the famous musicians. Barni describes King's colourful parties as : "Each night Khusrau brought new ghazals to the assembly of the king. Mohammad Shah, the famous musician of the time, played and beautiful dancing girls like Fatuha and Nusrat Khatun sang, 'bringing the birds down from the air and robbing the hearers of their senses', while the graceful dancing of Nusrat-Bibi and Mihir Afruz, their coquetish gestures and charming motions 'spilt a saltmine. on every side."[3] TheKing allotted a pension of 1,200 Tanghas annually. Alauddin Khilji (1296-1316 A.D.), the great patron of arts gave the best opportunities to Khusrau to develop his art of music and bestowed on him great honour. This was the most fruitful period for Khusrau. During this period, he became the disciple of famous saint Nizamuddin Auliya and spent most of his time in prayers and religious obligations, and wrote many poems in praise of his mystic teacher. Probably this was the time when Khusrau developed a great liking for the several forms of Indian music. But the King was not on very good terms with Sheikh Nizamuddin Auliya, and he discouraged the mystic saints. Khusrau went to Oudh, and on his return he heard the news of the death of Nizamuddin Auliya. His heart was broken, and according to a famous legend, hearing the sad event he rent his garments and blackened his face, and went to the side of the grave of Sheikh and recited the following lines in Hindi[4]

गोरी सोवे सेज पर मुंह पर डारे केस
चल खुसरो घर आपने रैन भई सब देस

Ghiasuddin Tughlaq treated Khusrau kindly, and Khusrau wrote Tughlaq Nama, an account of the victory of Ghiasuddin Tughlaq. A few months later Khusrau died in Hijri 725, and

1. Acharya Brahaspati : Musalman Aur Bhartiya Sangeet, p. 57.
2 Chand Khan : Mousiqui-e-Hazrat Amir Khusrau; p. 198.
3. Mirza, Waheed : The Life and Works of Amir Khusrau ; p. 79
4. See Naqi Mohammad Khan : Hayat Amir Khurau

was buried near the grave of Nizamuddin Auliya.

From the above statements, it is clear that there is no doubt about Khusrau's attainments in music. He himself says in Gharat-ul-Kamal :[1]

नज़म रा करदम सह द फतर दर बा तहरीर आमदे
इल्म मौसीकी सह दीगर बू दार बा दर बूद

He believed that his command over the art of music was in no way less than his excellence in poetry.

Khusrau's mind was highly imaginative and independent, and he enjoyed creating new forms in music and poetry. He broke away from the old traditions, and created new forms of music.

Having reviewed the life sketch of Amir Khusrau as given above, we may now examine how far the contention that he was the originator of Khayal can be sustained.

After a deep study of his life and works, we find that Amir Khusrau has been described by the historians as the innovator of several forms, but the name of Khayal does not find a significant place in such descriptions. We might notice that names of Ghazal, Naat and Qaul singers who were present during the time of Amir Khusrau have been mentioned by the historians, but none of them has mentioned the name of even a single Khayal singer. The other treatises like Tohfat-ul-Hind, Raag Darpan, Usulun-Naghmat-e-Asifi, Risala Zikr-e-Mughannian-e-Hindustan have also not given any noteworthy description of this form, while describing the innovations of Amir Khusrau. On the other hand, we find that Qawwali, Qaul, etc., are clearly identified as contributions of Khusrau. Specimens of such compositions are traceable even today. Popular Indian melodies such as Qawwali, Qaul are undoubtedly the inventions of Amir Khusrau which were designed to produce novelty in Sufi 'Sama' rituals in which he himself participated.[2]

The origin of Khayal can be traced to Qawwali style (a kind of devotional and mystic songs). It is also true that Qawwali of present time is totally different in form and structure from the Qawwali of the time of Amir Khusrau. In Qawwali, small improvisations in particular Raags were allowed, and the text

1. See Muslim Saqafat.
2. Athar Abbas Rizvi : A History of Sufism in India, p.172.

of the songs was based on mysticism. Qawwali's original form and structure were retained until the later part of the seventeenth century by the mystic saints. But gradually their influence began to decline due to its entrance into courts of Kings and musical sittings of Amirs. Consequently, it lost its spiritual and mystic content, which was replaced by artistic and decorative forms dominated by Shringar Ras. Possibly in course of time this new type of Qawwali gave rise to a new form, known as Khayal.

(2) **Sultan Hussain Sharqui**

Sultan Hussain Sharqui was enthroned in the year 1485 A.D. in Jaunpur after his brother Mohammad Shah. He made treaty with Bahlul Lodi. He was married to Alauddin's daughter Khujan Begum.

After proclaiming the title of Shah he started strengthening his military power and attacked Orissa. King Kapileshwar of Orissa surrendered and Hussain Shah returned to Jaunpur. After some time he decided to attack Gwalior. He surrounded the fort of Gwalior for many days but could not enter the fort. Ultimately, King Mansingh proposed a treaty, and presented him valuable gifts, horses, elephants, etc. In this way foundation of Sharqui's rule began to take deep roots and he was regarded a powerful king.

Hussain Shah deeply loved his wife Khujan Begum and acted under her influence. She often put pressure on Hussain Shah to attack Delhi. Thus Sultan Hussain Shah attacked Delhi five times, and was defeated by Sikandar Lodi.[1]

Hussain Shah was the last king of Sharqui rulers. In fact he was most fortunate to inherit a peaceful State and like his grandfather he spent a lot of time in the construction of buildings and encouraging art and culture. But is was his misfortune that in order to fulfil the wishes of his wife, he attacked Delhi several times and he became the cause of the decline of Sharqui rule.[2]

Sultan Hussain was a man of many testes, and he had a great liking for fine arts. He treated the learned musicians

1. Syed Iqbal Ahmad : Sharqui Rajya Jaunyur Ka Itihas, Shiraz Hind Prakashan Bhavan, Jaunpur, 1968, p. 232.
2. Inayat Khan Rasikh : Rissala Zikr-e-Mughannian-e-Hindustan, p. 2

with great respect and offered them generous patronage. He was himself highly knowledgeable about music. He had acquired understanding of music not merely for entertainment, but had attained a high degree of insight about the principles and techniques of music. He, therefore, assembled the top ranking musicians in his court. Based on his knowledge and understanding of music he used to experiment with various novel combinations of Raags. In recognition of his vast knowledge and competence in music, the people of his time gave him the title of Nayak.[1]

According to Raag Darpan and Tohfat-ul-Hind, Sultan Hussain Shah composed seventeen Raags. Out of these there were twelve varieties of Shyam, four varieties of Todi, and one variety of Asavari.

Following are the names of the Raags innovated by him :

Varieties of Shyam

(1) Gaud Shyam (2) Malhar Shyam (3) Bhopal Shyam (4) Kanhra Shyam (5) Suhu Shyam (6) Purvi Shyam (7) Ram Shyam (8) Megh Shyam (9) Basant Shyam (10) Berari Shyam (11) Karai Shyam (12) Gaund Shyam.

Varieties of Todi

(1) Jaunpuri Todi – It was a combination of Jaunpuri and Todi.

(2) Rama Todi—It was a combination of Ramkali and Todi.

(3) Rasooli Todi—It was a composition of Multani and Dhanasari.

(4) Bhalimi Todi—This was also composed by combining some Raag with Todi but it was less popular.

He innovated one variety of Asavari which he called Jaunpuri Asavari.[2]

There is no doubt that Hussain Shah was a great patron of fine arts and especially of music, but we have to examine what contribution he has made to the origin and development of Khayal. Following are the opinions of some of the musicologists in this connection.

1. Inayat Khan Rasikh : Risala Zikr-e-Mughannian-e-Hindustan.
2. Raag Darpan and Tohfat-ul-Hind.

The authors of Sarmaya-e-Ishrat, Maarifun-Naghmat, Ghubar-e-Khatir,Madan-ul-Mousiqi and many more medieval writers are of the opinion that Sultan Hussain Sharqui was a great master of the art of music and he was the founder father of Khayal style. This view has also been expressed by some of the western authors such as Capt Willard and Fox Strangeways. It is interesting to note that Inayat Khan Rasikh, in his Risala-e-Zikr-e-Mughannian-e-Hindustan, has mentioned the name of Qawwali instead of Khayal. According to him "Sultan Hussain was an expert singer of Qawwali and some of his compositions are available in Khairabadi language".[1]

But a different school of musicians has questioned this viewpoint. According to Pt. V.N. Bhatkhande; "It is not correct to believe that any single person could have originated and developed the Khayal style. It is likely that musical compositions similar to Khayal already existed in the society, but they did not have due recognition and appreciation by the people at that time. Later, in the fifteenth century Sultan Hussain Sharqui took a fancy for it and encouraged the musicians to sing in this style, which might have given impetus to its development and popularity".[2]

According to Acharya Brihaspati : "The independent ruler Ibrahim Sharqui (1402-1440 A.D.) was a very knowledgeable person. Sultan Hussain Shah, who also belonged to Sharqui dynasty, was a great connoisseur of music and also a contemporary of Mansingh Tanwar of Gwalior. Famous singers like Ghooran (period of Babur), Sheikh Adhan (famous Sufi musician) and Sheikh Bhanju (who once challenged Tansen in Akbar's court), were all from Jaunpur. Thus, all these artistes from Jaunpur were called Qawwal Bachchay, and they were always in conflict with the Kalawants. Kalawants believed that Khayal singers have destroyed the purity of Raags.[3]

Another modern musicologist, Swami Prajnananda is of the opinion that "Sharqui rulers were great lovers as well as patrons of fine arts like Architecture, painting and music, and so

1. Inayat Khan Rasikh : Risala-e-Zikr-e-Mughannian-e-Hindustan, p. 24.
2. Bhatkhande Sangeet Shastra-I; p. 55.
3. Sulochna and Acharya Brihaspati : 'Khayal'; Sangeet, July, 1979.

it can be assumed that Khayal got their support and it was much improved and better understood during the time of Sultan Hussain Sharqui".[1]

Thakur Jaidev Singh has dealt with this subject in considerable detail, and is of the opinion that Sultan Hussain Sharqui can not be said to be the originator of this style. He states that the style of Khayal was ornate and romantic and it did not find favour in the temples. It was mostly patronized by the Kathiks, the dancing girls, and kings. The Sharqui Kings of Jaunpur patronized this style to a great extent. He further states that "there was a certain style of musical composition, and certain style of rendering already prevalent in music, and Khayal was only a natural development of that style".[2]

The foregoing analysis of the different viewpoints and biographies of Amir Khusrau and Sultan Hussain Sharqui reveals that the emergence of Khayal as a style of music can not be attributed to the contribution of any single personality. A study of our ancient Shastric texts will indicate that the roots of Khayal were already present in our ancient musical system. The modern musicologists have attempted to prove this point by referring to our monumental Sanskrit texts like Sangeet Ratnakar of Sarangdev, and Brihaddeshi of Matanga. In these texts some styles of singing have been described, the structure of which resembles with the Khayal style. Given below are some illustrations of these viewpoints :

Among the three varieties of Nibaddha Gaan described in Sangeet Ratnakar (Prabandha, Vastu, Rupak), dramatic situation plays an important role in Rupak. It is interesting to note, as has been mentioned earlier, that some Lavni (a folk song) singers describe in their songs the historical stories and play Chhang (an instrument) and their songs are called Khayal. While describing Rupak, Maharana Kumbha in his book Sangeet Raj has mentioned that dramatic situation plays an important role in it. On this basis we find a similarity between Rupak and Khayal of Lavni singers. Secondly, Rupak refers

1. Swami Prajnananda : A Historical Study of Idian Music, p. 213.
2. Thakur Jaidev Singh : 'The Evolution of Khayal', Commemoration Volume in Honour of Dr. S. N. Ratanjankar, 1961, pp. 127-132.

to drama in Hindi language which has visual implications. These characteristics of Rupak are traceable in Khayal of folk singers as well as in musical dramas.

Pt. Sarangdev has described Rupak Prabandha in the following words :

गुणान्वितं दोषदीनं नवं रुपकमुत्तमम्
रागेण धातुकातुभ्यां तथा ताललयौडुवै :
नूतनै रुपकं नूत्मं रागः स्थायान्तरैर्नवः
धातुरागांशभेदेन मातोस्तु नवता भवेत्
प्रतिपाद्यविशेषेण रसालंकारभेदतः
लयग्रहविशेषेण तालानां नवता मता
ताल विश्रामवोऽन्येन विश्रामेण लयो नवः
छन्दोगणग्रहन्यासप्रत्रन्धावयवैर्नवैः
औडुवापरपर्याया रचना नवतां व्रजेत

On the basis of above description, it can be said that Rupak Prabandha is a kind of composition which is novel and original in conception. The new forms of compositions, rhythm, tempo, etc. are designed with different metres, aesthetic sentiments, and mood.[1]

While comparing Khayal with Rupak Prabandha, Pt. S.N. Ratanjankar states : "Rupakam, a type of songs, referred to in the old Granthas, appears to have in it the germs of the Khayal style. Rupakam is a musical composition in which there is scope for creating novelty, something original out of the trodden path in the Raag as well as in the wordings of the composition by emphasizing passages which, though ordinarily occurring in the Raag being sung are prominent in some other sympathetic Raag, by using fresh words expressing some emotions, by making changes in the Tala and Laya. It may not be too fantastic perhaps to consider the Khayal as an off shoot of the Rupakam type of musical compositions. Within a short time after Sarangdev, the old system of music was receding in the background and a new one in which influence of foreign music was beiginning to rush in, was coming into vogue".[2]

1. Swami Prajnananda : A Historical Study of Indian Music, p. 207.
2. Ibid., p. 207.

Some scholars connect the evolution of Khayal to Shastrik Akshiptika, which was a kind of Nibaddha Gaan pertaining to Margi Sangeet. It was a composition which was sung with the help of Tala, Svara, and Pada such as Chanchat-puta Tal which seems to be a variety of Marga Talas. Different varieties of Akshiptika have been described in Sangeet Ratnakar. Some musicologists are of the opinion that the musical composition is set in a particular Raag-Tal, and also contains Pada, the literary content. In this manner it embodies all the elements of Khayal style.

Apart from the above opinions, the most noteworthy thought is that the origin of Khayal style may be related to our ancient Geetis, particularly to Sandharani Geeti. Geeti was considered the system or manner involved in the style of musical composition and rendering. In ancient Shastras five types of Geetis have been mentioned in the context of five varieties of Gram Raags :

गीतय: पश्च शुद्धा च भिन्ना गौडी च वैसरासाधारणीति

Shuddha referred to the type of Raag composition in which the arrangement of notes was straight and graceful. In Bhinna the arrangement and movement of notes were crooked, and the pronunciation of notes was characterized by sweet and subtle Gamakas. The tones of Gaudi were brought and knit together in three octaves, and it was also full of Gamakas. Versa referred to the Veg Svara (Rapid movement of notes), its movements covered all the three octaves, and the notes were uttered in quick tempo. Sadharani Geeti has been described by Pt. Sarangdev in the following manner :

चतुर्गीति गतं लक्ष्माश्रिता साधारणीतिमता

It was a composite style which incorporated the characteristics of all the other four styles. Matanga has described seven instead of five varieties of Geetis. But regarding Sadharani Geeti, he also agrees that it was based on the beautiful combination of all the Geetis. This means that the scope of Sadharani is very much wider and comprehensive. Khayal style seems to contain the characteristics of Sadharani Geeti, because various embellishments permissible in Sadharani Geeti are employed in Khayal. According to Thakur Jaidev Singh : "I maintain that so called Khayal style of musical composition is nothing but only a development of Sadharani Geeti which used the exquisite features of all the styles. It is this Sadharani Geeti with the predominant use of Bhinna in it that became Khayal. Such styles of musical compositions have been in existence in Indian music at least from seventh and eighth centuries A.D. The Sadharani style of composition with generous and plentiful use of Gamaks became our Khayal composition".[1]

It may be clarified here that the word composition has been used by the author not in the sense of only the closed compositional forms indicated by terms like Prabandha; it embraces the entire structure of arrangement and movement of musical notes in the delineation of different Raags. The most important characteristic of Khayal style is Alapti or Raag elaboration. Alapti brings forth the depth of feelings and sentiments, and it highlights the creative imagination with the help of Gamak, Varna, Alankar, and elaboration of small phrases (Sthayas). Pt. Sarangdev describes Alapti in the following manner :

वर्णालंकार सम्पन्ना गमकस्थायचित्रिता ।
आलप्ति रूच्यते तज्ज्ञैर्भूरिभंगिमनोहरा ।।

Two types of Alapti have been described, namely, Raagaapati and Rupakalapti. In the context of Khayal, a discussion of Rupakalapti is more relevant. Pt. Sarangdev has given the definition of Rupakalapti as follows :

रूपकस्थेन रागेण तालेन च विधीयते ।
या प्रोक्ता रूपकालप्तिः सा पुनर्द्विविधा भवेत् ।।
प्रतिग्रहणिकैकान्या भंजनीत्यभिधीयते ।
विधाय स्थायमालप्ते रूपकावयो यदि ।।
प्रतिगृह्येत सा प्रोक्ता प्रतिग्रहणिका बुधैः ।
भंजनी द्विविधा ज्ञेया स्थायरूपकभंजनात् ।।
यदा तत्पदमानेन स्थायो रूपकसंस्थितः ।
नानाप्रकारः क्रियते सा ज्ञेया स्थायभंजनी ।।
तैः पदैस्तेन मानेन समग्रं रूपकं यदि ।
अन्यथा चान्यथा गायेदसौ रूपकभंजनी ।।

1. **Thakur Jaidev Singh : 'The Evolution of Khayal', loc. cit., pp. 127-132.**

The variety of Alapti which has a tonal relevance to the Raag and Taal of a particular composition is called Rupakalapti. It has been divided into two parts :

(1) **Pratigrahnika**—This is incorporated in between the composition, and has to conform to the Raag and Tala. When after singing a phrase in accordancc with the Raag, it is joined with tbe totality of the composition, it is called Pratigrahnika. The description of Pratigrahnika resembles the process of rendering some Alap in Khayal style, and joining it with the small phrase of the composition, that is Mukhra (refrain).

(2) **Bhanjani**—Bhanjani, the second variety of Rupakalapti, has been further divided into two categories : (i) Sthaya Bhanjani (ii) Rupak Bhanjani

It is interesting to note that all the qualities which have been described in our ancient books regarding these two varieties of Bhanjani are comparable to our present system of elaborating the small phrases in Khayal style. Kallinatha, the commentator of Ratnakar, has described Sthaya Bhanjani in the following manner :

नाना प्रकार: विचित्ररीतियुक्त: क्रियते

गातृवादकप्रतिभाविशेषेणोभ्दाव्यतेचैत्सा स्थायभंजनी

Keeping in view the above definition, Sthaya Bhanjani refers to the recitation of a small phrase of musical composition in varied, novel and artistic ways which provides opportunities to the musician, to display his imagination, creativity, and skill. We might notice here that in Khayal the singers adopt this technique when they take up a small phrase of the composition and develop it beautifully in various ways.

In Rupak Bhanjani the Sthayas were placed by suitable Gamaks, the Tanas were also a part of it. As described by Pt. Sarangdev in Rupak Bhanjani the musician is not tied down to the Tanas occurring only in the composition that he is singing, but also uses other Tanas appropriate to that particular Raag embellished with Gamak, etc.[1]

Some scholars and writers have also associated Khayal with the Karnatak form Pallavi, which comes in the branch of Manodharma Sangeet, and is the largest item in South Indian

1. Thakur Jaidev Singh : 'The Evolution of Khayal', loc. cit.

concerts. It contributes greatly to its academic and aesthetic value. In Pallavi the musician has ample opportunities of displaying his creative talents, imaginative skill, artistic sense, and musical intelligence.[1]

The description and analysis of the various viewpoints given above lead us to the conclusion that Khayal is a novel form of music which has absorbed diverse influences from the various musical traditions and it becomes an untenable proposition to consider it as the creation of one person's genius. The genesis of Khayal can be traced to the eighth century A.D. when a number of musical forms and compositions were already in existence which had some of the characteristics similar to Khayal. Meanwhile, a series of Muslim invasions brought new influences in the society, culture and artistic pursuits. The blending of the Indian culture with the cultural influences brought in by Muslims from Persia, Central Asia and Arab countries led to the emergence of several new patterns in all fields of fine arts, especially in in the field of architecture, painting and music. A fine example of the blend of various influences is found in the genius of some outstanding persons, such as Amir Khusrau in the thirteenth century. He was a man of extraordinary merit and intelligence, and was well-versed in the Indian languages. Since he was a lover of Indian music and a scholar of great learning, he must have been aware of the compositions described in our ancient Shastrik texts. It is also noteworthy that the various ancient compositions were described in Sangeet Ratnakar which was written around the same period, which is a further evidence of the continuity of ancient traditions during the time of Khusrau.

Sufi saints utilized music for their religious Samas (assemblies), in which Qaul style became popular and was transformed into Qawwali. Amir Khusrau had a particular liking for Qawwali and he composed hundres of songs in this style.

In this process, the ancient Shastrik Prabandha, Raag Geeti, and Rupakalapti were influenced by the styles like Qawwali, etc. and it culminated in the emergence of a new style of music which came to be known as Khayal. But it did

1. Sambamoorty : South Indian Music; Part IV, Ch. II.

not attain much popularity, as indicated by the absence of any mention of Khayal as a style of music in the Granthas of that time, and could not find a proper place in the Moghul court until the end of the first century. Meanwhile, Sharqui Kings of Jaunpur took keen interest in the development and popularization of this style. However, during the fifteenth and sixteenth centuries this style did not get much encouragement. The main reason for its oblivion was the dominance of Dhruvapad during that period because of which it was not given patronage in the royal court and the musical form of high standard by the elite. In this connection it may also be noted that in Ain-e-Akbari, Abul Fazl has described mostly the names of Kalawants (Dhruvapad singers) while he has not mentioned the names of Qawwal (Khayal singers).

Another viewpoint to explain the lesser significance of Khayal style during that period is that all the Muslim singers belonged to one section of society called Mirasis. They were called Kalawants in the courts of Kings and Rajahs. In the musical assemblies of the Sufi saints they were known as Qawwals, and the Sikhs described them as Rababis. The Qawwals associated with the Sufi saints confined themselves exclusively to the devotional music. They never sang Qawwali, Qaul, Qalbanas and other musical compositions containing sacred names of God, prophets and religious saints in the court of Kings because they considered it humiliating to recite such holy names for the entertainment of the rulers seated on the higher pedestals. The Kings themselves were conscious of this feeling and, therefore, avoided the recital of such songs in their courts.[1]

A detailed analysis of the works of the period under study indicates that Khayal was much more popular and understood during the seventeeth and eighteenth centuries. In Tohfat-ul-Hind, the topic of Khayal has been discussed soon after Dhruvapad and Vishnupad. According to the author of Tohfat-ul-Hind, "Khayal contains two Tuks (verses) and most of the compositions of this period are in Khairabadi language". The

32. Ustad Chand Khan : Mousiqi Hazrat Amir Khusrau; p. 187.

author has incorporated Tappa, Chutkala, and Purbi as parts of the description of Khayal.

In Raag Darpan also we find the description of Khayal immediately after Dhruvapad. The author says : "Khayal is sung in the contemporary language of Delhi. Usually it consists of two verses, but some of its compositions contain four verses also. The first two verses make a set, and the next two verses constitute a different set".

In Usul un-Naghmat-e-Asifi, Khayal style has not been described in detail. The author has mentioned Khayal as a form of Desi Sangeet. Possibly the reason for not discussing it in detail may be that the author of the book has mainly concentrated on the subject of classification of Raag and other technical points, and has given lesser space to the description of forms and styles prevalent during his period. But Hakim Mohammad Karam Imam, who wrote Madan-ul-Mousiqi during the nineteenth century, has described the popularity of Khayal style during his period. The author states : "Sultan Hussain Sharqui of Jaunpur has composed a style of singing in Khairabadi language with great maturity, beauty and aesthetic excellence, which has come to be known as Khayal. This style is very popular among the present musicians"[1]

The political instability during the eighteenth century drove many musicians from the capital to the smaller States. In this process Khayal style took a new turn and the mystic elements in it began to be substituted by artistic and aesthetic forms in musical compositions. This new development was considerably instrumental in the popularity of Khayal during the eighteenth century. During the same period a musician known as Niyamat Khan in the court of Mohammad Shah played an important role in promoting the Khayal style. According to Inayat Khan Rasikh, Niyamat Khan was one of the greatest singers of the Dhruvapad, Khayal and Tarana styles, and he composed several Khayals with a high degree of perfection.[2] In his com-

1. Hakim Mohammad Karam Imam : Madan-ul-Mousiqi, p. 162.

2. Inayat Khan Rasikh : Risala Zikr-e-Mughannian-e-Hindustan, p. 30.

positions his name has been given as Sadarang.[1] His Khayals acquired such popularity that even today the musicians recite them, and use them as a model for new compositions. Following are two examples of his compositions, one of these is based on devotional and mystic sentiments while the other is based on aesthetic and romantic sentiments :

(1) राग दरबारी

तुम साईं करीम, रहीम, हकीम पाक परवरदिगार
गरबी को गरब दूर कर डारत एक छिन में
दुखियन को मोरे दाता
जो मो मन की इच्छा हो सो पुजिवो साहेब
सदारंग को दीजे दीन दुखी के दाता

(2) राग सूर मल्हार

आये गरजत बादरवा, अति ही सुहाए
रूमझूम चहुं और ते बरसे
सदारंग अति ही सुख पाये

Firoze Khan, who has been described as the nephew, son-in-law, and disciple of Sadarang, and is known by the title of Adarang, was also an accomplished composer of Khayals of similar style.[2] Following is one example of his compositions :

राग नट मल्हार

ऐ सुहागपरी कारी बदरिया
बरसन लागी अति जोर
अदारंग बूंद फुहार परन लागी
कैसे मिलूं चितचोर

Niyamat Khan Sadarang and other perceptive musicians of that time analysed the reasons for the ascendance of Dhruvapad and unpopularity of Khayal. They endeavoured to incorporate the characteristics of Dhruvapad into Khayal in which they were successful. As a result, Khayal gained acceptance and appreciation in the royal courts. Gradually this style acquired a place of great eminence in the court as well as a wide popularity among all classes of society due to its unique

1. Further details of Sadarang are given in the last section of this study.

2. See Dargah Quli Khan : Muraqqa-e-Dehli.

and artistic appeal. The musicians of that time started acquiring perfection in it and introduced many innovations and experimentations to please the kings and rulers. In a book entitled Muraqqa-e-Dehli which was written soon after the invasion of Nadirshah, a detailed description of famous musicians of Delhi is given. Among these singers the majority of names are of Khayal and Qawwali singers, and very few names of Dhruvapad singers. Some of the names of the Khayal singers described in this book are : Kamal Bai, Razi, Qasim Ali, Panna Bai, Rahim Khan, Jahani, Khawasi and Anutha, Allah Bande, Daulat Khan and Uma Bai.[1]

1. Khwaja Hasan Nizami : Purani Dehli Ke Halaat.

CHAPTER VII

Other Forms and Styles

IN the first two chapters of this Section we have discusse the origin and development of the two major forms of Hintustani Music, namely, Dhruvapad and Khayal, which are very well known and are sung and appreciated at present in select gatherings of classical music in north India. In this chapter, we shall describe several other forms and styles of Hindustani Music prevalent during the seventeenth and eighteenth centuries, some of which are still popular, such as Tarana and Qawwali, but most of which have become obscure, such as Naqsh-Gui, Nigar, Baseet, etc., and there are very few people, who are competent at present to perform such styles of music. We have also found mention of some forms and styles in the literature of this period which are almost unknown now, such as Suraj Prakash, Chandra Prakash, Dhva, Matha, Jhoomra, etc. These have also been described briefly.

Tarana

Tarana refers to a form of singing these days in which certain selected syllables devoid of meaning are repetitively interwoven and recited in any Raag. At present this form does not have any individual identity of its own, and is generally treated as a part of Khayal style. But an analysis of its historical past reveals that it was a distinct and advanced style of music having its own important place in the musical system as indicated in the important works written during the medieval period.

The origin of Tarana is generally associated with the innovations of Amir Khusrau. The authors of the following books have also indentified Amir Khusrau as the originator of this style : 1. Tohfat-ul-Hind; 2. Raag Darpan; 3. Madan-ul-Mousiqi; 4. Naghmat-ul-Hind; 5. Maarifun-Naghmat.

In Tohfat-ul-Hind, written during the eighteenth century, it is stated that "the Indians call Tarana as Tillana. These are Arabic and Persian couplets in which few meaningless syllables are repeated in various melodious forms. The principles and structure of this style have been derived from Hindustani Geet".[1]

Although the recitation and repetition of meaningless syllables as a part of singing was in vogue since the time of Bharata's Natyashastra, which is generally considered as a work of fifth century A.D. Among the various varieties of Geets described in this work, Nirgeet has been mentioned as a type of Geet based on some meaningless syllables. Narada is considered the innovator of this Geet. According to Pt. N. Sarangdev, following are few syllables of ancient Shushkaksharas (meaningless syllables) :

इण्टुं जगतिपि वल्लिकित कुचझल तितिझल
पशुपति दिगिदिगि वादिगोंग गणपति तितिधा

In the Natyashastra of Bharata, Chhands of meaningless syllables are also found. For example :

दिग्ले दिग्ले झं टुं झं टूं जं बुक वतिलक तेत्तेनाम्

It is noteworthy that these syllables were not altogether meaningless. In between the syllables, the names of gods like Ganpati, Pashupati, etc., were also included. Among the six Angas of Prabandha described in Sangeet Ratnakar, Tenak is also formed by combining such syllables.

It is interesting to note that the author of Tohfat-ul-Hind has considered Tarana and Tillana as equal terms. Tillana, which is a part of singing in Karnatak style of music is sung as a form of composition, and is also sung as accompaniment to dance. But Tarana has been associated with the Khayal style of Hindustani Music, and is considered an integral part of vocal music.

The noteworthy consideration in this connection is that whereas the structure and form of Tarana today have been

1. Tohfat-ul-Hind, edited by N. H. Ansari.

reduced to a decorative pattern for the Khayal style, in the original form it was not merely a composition of meaningless syllables. Tarana at that stage included the Persian and Arabic couplets and Rubaiyat, which were decorated with few syllables like Ta, Re, Da, Ni, De, Re, etc.[1] It had a unique and distinct place in Hindustani music system. An examination of such songs leads us to agree with the opinion that Tarana must have started developing during Amir Khusrau's time.

The question before us, howeve, is whether Amir Khusrau originated this style with his own imagination, or there existed some such compositions in the Arabic and Persian systems of music. It is interesting to note that in the Arabic music there was mention of a form of singing called Nauba, even before the tenth century A.D. Nauba was based on four parts, and one of these was Tarana. Such compositions have also been identified before Abdur-Qadir Rabn-e-Ghaibi (1435 A.D.). Even today in Andalusia (a province in Spain) Tarana is the name of a kind of dance and singing and it is performed aceording to the classical style.

In the light of the above discussion, it may be said that a form of music similar to Tarana existed in the Arabic music even though its structure was different from Hindustani Tarana. Thus it would be difficult to support the argument that Tarana was developed entirely by Amir Khusrau's imagination. On the other hand, it would be more appropriate to say that his contribution was to introduce this form in Hindustani music on the basis of similar existing patterns in the ancient Hindustani and other musical systems.

Amir Khusrau had composed several such Taranas which conveyed full meaning. For example, the following Tarana is popular even today among the musicians :[2]

स्थाई

दर आ दर आ जाने मन दर आ दर आ

दिर तनम दर आ दर आ

1. Rashid Malik : Hazrat Amir Khusrau ka Ilm-e-Mousiqui aur Doosre Maqalaat; p. 184. vide Farmer : The Sources of Arabian Music, London; 1965-XIX.

2. Naqi Mohammad Khan : Hayat Amir Khusrau; p. 201.

अंतरा

बतंग आमदम चन्द इन्तजार कराम

बया-बया कि तरा तंग दर किनार कशम

Amir Khusrau has utilized Qaul form of singing in his several Taranas. Following is an example in which the Arabic words have been used in its Antara :[1]

स्थाई

है या दिर दिर ताला लाले हसन वो निज़ामुद्दीन औलिया

दीं तीं दिर दिर दिर तिले ता ना ना ना ना ना ना ना

अन्तरा

फ़इन्नुमा तवल्लुकसमा वजहिल्ला दिर तूँ

तोम तन न न दिर ने

तिल्ले दरा जानं दीं दीं दिर दिर दिर

ता ना तिल्ले त न न न न।

In the same pattern, a popular Tarana of Amir Khusrau composed in Raag Suha and Farodast Taal is given below :

स्थाई

द रा तेले दा नी अमशल लाये अमशल लाये तेला यले

अन्तरा

बर नदी व बशोखी हमचू खुसरो

हजारां खानुमा बरफन्दा बाशी

Although this style was introduced sometime in the fourteenth century, it did not acquire as much recognition in the royal courts, but it was popular in musical sittings of Sufis and religious assemblies on Mazars (tombs of saints). Like Khayal, it became popular among all classes of musicians in the later half of seventeenth and eighteenth centuries. At this stage Tarana consisted of the songs of lighter mood, and gradually it became a part of Khayal style. Several such Taranas are found in Nadirat-e-Shahi, which was written during the time of Shah Alam. A closer scrutiny of these songs reveals that Tarana consisted of Urdu couplets also along with Persian Rubaiyat during that period. Following are two examples :

1. Ghulam Rasul : 'Sada Bahar Gayan Shaili : Tarana' : Sangeet, January, 1968.

(1) तराना राग सारंग (चलता तिताला)
दीम दीम त ना दिरना तारी दानी ओदिना
त ना दिर ना तारे दानी
जमाना नेस्त बयक रंग ऐ दिला बिशुनौ
बदोस्तानी अदू खसलत आशना तु मशौ

(2) तराना राग भूपाली (बंधा तिताला)
तोम ताना दिर ना तरे दानी ता दानी दिरना दीम तारे दानी
हर एक गुनाह की परवरदिगार तौबः ।
कीजे कबूल मेरी ऐ किर्दगार तौबः ।।

The large number of Taranas in Nadirat-e-Shahi is a clear evidence of the fact that Tarana had become an important form of the court music. At the same time Tarana was widely sung in the gatherings of Sufi saints, who brought in many changes and improvisations in this style, according to the changing atmosphere of that time. For example, the Tarana composed by Khwaja Sayed Hasan Rasul-e-Ima during the time of Aurangzeb :[1]

स्थाई
दिर दा जाने मन तोम ता ना ना दिर दिर दानी
तुम दिर दिर तानी ता दा रे दानी

अन्तरा
गरकुए नेकनामी मारा गुज़र न दादन
गर तू नमी पसन्दीं ता ग़ैर कुन कज़ारा
ताना ना दिर दिर दानी तुं दिर दिर दानी ता दा रे दा नी ।

A story is associated with this Tarana that it was composed by a Sufi saint. It is believed that during Aurangzeb's time, eunuchs of Delhi came to know about the Emperor's order to eliminate them by putting them on a boat which was to be sunk, as the Emperor thought that they were useless and a bad influence on the community. The eunuchs are believed to have approached the Sufi saint who composed this Tarana, the meaning of which is that : "O emperor; if we are so unwanted by the society, then change our fate instead of killing us". On hearing this Tarana the emperor spared their life.[2]

1. Ustad Chand Khan : 'Tarana Gayaki Ki Visheshtayen', Sangeet, Jan., 1968.
2. Ibid.

A study of Tarana of that time points out that three types of Taranas were in vogue :

(1) Compositions having the syllables of Tarana in the Sthayi as well as in Antara.

(2) Compositions having the Tarana syllables in the Sthayi, and Persian and Urdu couplets in the Antara.

(3) Compositions having Tarana syllables in the Sthayi, and syllables of Trivat in the Antara. In this style the vocalists and accompanists used to engage in artistic competition. In some books such style has been mentioned as Tulan.[1] An example of such Tarana is given below :

[स्थाई]

ता ना दे रे दे रे ता ना दे रे ता दा रे दा नीं ना दिर दिर ना
दिर दिर तुम दिर दिर धेतलान् तुम दिर दिर धेतलान् तुम दिर दिर

अन्तरा

या ला ली या ला ली चा ला लोम या ला लोम या ली या ली
किड़नक धिरकिट लक धिरकिट तक धा कड़ान धा
गदगिन धा गदगिन धा

Another important composer of Taranas was Mian Kutab Bakhsh, whose title was Tanaras Khan, and he belonged to the last period of Mughal empire. He has composed hundreds of artistic Taranas. Following is an example of his Tarana compositions :

स्थाई

दा नी दिर या दारा तद रे दा नी ना दिर दिर दा नी
तुम दिर दिर दानी त दरे दा नी तुम दिर दिर
ता दा रे दा नी ता अदानी

अन्तरा

मुक़ाबिला भी अपच का कहो तो दस में लूं
तराना ऐसा सुनाऊं कि तानरस में लूं ।

The foregoing analysis of the various stages through which Tarana has passed reveals that Tarana was a form of music having its own unique and important place among the styles of music, particularly during the seventeenth and eighteenth

1. Ustad Chand Khan : 'Tarana Gayaki Ki Kuchh Visheshtayen', Sangeet, Jan., 1968, p. 86.

centuries. The three manuscripts of that period which have been discussed in the first section of the study also indicate the significance of this style as an independent popular form of music.

Qawwali

Qawwali is a popular form of music even today, but it was in vogue as far back as the thirteenth and fourteenth century A.D. It has undergone many changes since its origin at different stages. The form today is quite different from what it used to be in its early stages. At present generally a group of four, five or more persons sing together in a Qawwali performance. The Talas used in Qawwali are also of particular type, which are seldom used in the classical music. The songs chosen for Qawwali usually are the couplets in Persian, Urdu or Hindi which are composed in a particular Raag.

According to the scholars who have traced the history of Qawwali, the singers of Qaul were called Qawwals. Over a period of time the shape of Qaul underwent changes, and a form similar to it started emerging which was called Qawwali.[1] It is likely that along with the shape of Qaul, its subject matter has also changed. Qaul referred to the Arabic Rubais in praise of gods and prophets sung in a particular style. In course of time the Rubai was replaced by Ghazal, and thus Qawwali became different from Qaul both in form and content. In its early stages, when Qawwali was a part of Arabian music, it was considered to be a composite of five parts : (1) Qaul (2) Ghazal (3) Tarana (4) Farodast (5) Mistzad.[2]

People in general associate Qawwali with Amir Khusrau. Maulana Mohammad Hussain Azad in his book Ab-e-Hayat confirms this belief and states : "Qawwali is the innovation of Amir Khusrau and is sung on the pattern laid down by him. It was on account of this contribution that Sultan-ul-Mashaikh gave him the title of Muftah-us-Samah. However, if we search the historical development of this form minutely, we will find that the above mentioned viewpoint is not supported by facts. As far back as the tenth century, a style of singing somewhat

1. Rashid Malik : Hazrat Amir Khusrau Ka Ilm-e-Mousiqi Aur Doosre Maqalat; p. 182-184.

2. Ibid, p. 182-184

similar to Qawwali was found among the Arab musicians in which small groups of singers used to participate and sing together. A description of such a style is traceable in the book Al-Aghani of Abul Faraj Ali Bin-As-Hussain-Bin Mohammad-Al-Qarshi-Al-Asfahani (A.D. 896-97). This book gives us the clue that groups of singers used to form small teams, who participated in the singing one after the other in sequence. Such groups of singers were called Nauba in Arabic. In due course the term Nauba was associated with the form of music sung by such groups. The Nauba style of singing had already come into existence before the tenth century A.D.[1]

According to another point of view, the Sufi saints in medieval India practised music regularly, and they used to convey their mystic message through music.[2] Much before Amir Khusrau, the famous disciple of Sheikh Hamiduddin Nagauri, known Qawwal Mahmood had created a sensation in the court of Shamsuddin Iltutmish (1210-1235 A.D.).[3] Sheikh Hamiduddin was a disciple of Khwaja Moinuddin Chishti of Ajmer.

Qawwali has been an integral part of the mystic, religious, and cultural gatherings of Indian Muslims. It is said that the famous mystic saint Sheikh Qutbuddin Bakhtiar Kaki (1236 A.D.) expired while listening to Qawwali. About Sheikh Nizamuddin Chishti, it has been stated that he often used to dance in ecstasy while listening to Qawwali. Sometimes he used to remain in a trance for several days, as a result of such musical sittings.[2]

In Ghunyat-ul-Munya (1374-75 A.D.) a description of the characteristics for Qawwals and their voices has been given. Following are some of these characteristics :[3]

(1) He should be familiar with the style of Geet and Raags.

(2) He should have a control on the ascending and descending notes.

(3) His voice should neither be too harsh nor too soft.

(4) He should take all possible care to protect the quality of his voice.

1. Acharya Brahaspati : 'Bhartiya Sangeet Ke Param Bhakt Amir Khusrau', Sangeet, 1976.
2. Acharya Brihaspati : Musalman Aur Bhartiya Sangeet : p. 28.
3. Ghunyat-ul-Munya, edited by Shahab Sarmadee, p. 109.

In Ghunyat-ul-Munya it has been suggested that the group of Qawwals must include some female singers also because the combination and contrast of their voices with those of the male singers leads to heightened impact and greater beauty in Qawwali. Regarding the female singers for the Qawwali group it has been suggested that they should be young and good looking maidens, possessing good quality of voice.

By the end of fourteenth century, the mystic and religious content of Qawwali began to decline. Meanwhile a new form influenced by Qawwali, called Khayal, developed with a changed perspective which was dominated by romantic and artistic compositions, and the Khayal singers began to be called Qawwals. Qawwali was thus associated with the Khayal style. As the popularity of Khayal increased, the structure of Qawwali changed. Abul Fazl has described Qawwals as Dhadhis, who used to sing Kadhka songs in the battlefields. At this stage Persian songs became the integral part of Qawwali.[1] Qawwali continued in these forms until the time of Bahadurshah Zafar, the last Moghul Emperor. Since Persian was not understood by the common man, the Sufis adopted the Hindi language, and they introduced Hindi words and couplets also in Qawwali.[2]

The musicians in the court of Mohammad Shah (1719-1746 A.D.) made a great deal of contribution to the development of Khayal : along with it Qawwali also grew and became a more melodious and attractive form of music. Women singers too started taking interest and participated in Qawwali.[3] At this stage the influence of saints and Sufis on Qawwali style was faded and it was sung almost in the same manner as Khayal.

Qawwali has not been described separately in the three manuscripts which have been examined in detail in the earlier chapters of this study, whereas Qaul and Qalbana have been described in considerable detail. This phenomenon has been interpreted by some authors as an indication of the approach in which the following styles are considered to be the various

1. Acharya Brihaspati : Musalman Aur Bhartiya Sangeet, p. 28.
2. Ibid., p. 26
3. Goswami, Premchand : 'Qawwali Katha' ; Sangeet, Jul., 1979.

components of the large structure of Qawwali : (1) Qaul (2) Qalbana (3) Naqsh (4) Gul (5) Nigar (6) Baseet (7) Rang (8) Ghazal.

All the abovementioned forms have been described in the various manuscripts and books of the seventeenth and eighteenth centuries. Each of these styles has been described briefly in the following pages.

Qaul

Qaul is one of the well known musical forms of the later medieval period. The word Qaul has been derived from the Arabic word Qaulah. It means to speak or to give an opinion. Qaul referred to a poetic composition in which some saying of prophet Mohammad or a verse from holy Quran was incorporated, in a particular Raag. In other words, the idea was to transform an Arabic prose into a musical form without distorting its meaning. Since it was not always possible to do so, a few syllables of Tarana were added to balance the Raag in which the piece was composed.[1]

It also consists of two parts : Sthayi and Antara. Occassionally a few Persian words are also used, which have a mystic thought. Qalbana, Naqsh, Gul, etc., are considered to be different categories of Qaul. A particular type of Taal is played for Qaul which is called Qawwali.[2]

Faqueerullah in his Raag Darpan has stated that Qaul is an innovation of Amir Khusrau. It may be noted that he refers to a famous incident in which Amir Khusrau had surpassed the well known singer Gopal Nayak in South by composing Qauls in response to the Geets of Gopal Nayak. According to Faqueerullah :

"Gopal Nayak came to Delhi during the period of Sultan Alauddin to compete with Amir Khusrau. He had tied a Dandi on his head (Dandi refers to a piece of wood about a foot long which is tied in the turban, it was symbolic of a person's challenge for competition). Amir Khusrau informed Alauddin : "A renowned musician Gopal Nayak is coming, accompanied by his twelve hundred disciples. His

1. Akbarabadi, Maikash : 'Qawwali', in Mousiqi Number of Aaj Kal, 1956.

2. Raja Nawab Ali : Maarifun-Naghmat.

throne is being carried by his disciples. I request you to hide me underneath your throne and invite Gopal to sing in your court. Please tell him that Amir is unwell, and until he recovers you will sing in the court". Gopal sang for six days, and Amir remained hidden underneath the throne. On the seventh day, Amir came to the court with two groups of his disciples, namely : Samit and Tatars. When Gopal asked him to sing Amir replied : 'I have just returned from Iran, and I am not such a high ranking artiste who can tie a Dandi to his head. I have learnt music merely as a hobby, and as a source of entertainment. I request you to sing first, then I shall sing whatever I am capable of". Gopal started singing, and regarding each of his songs Khusrau said : "I had already composed such a song long ago". He then sang Qaul and Baseet composed by him in the same style in response to Gopal's Geet. Gopal was astonished. Later, Amir sang some of his original compositions of Qaul, etc.".[1]

Although this story indicates that Amir Khusrau was highly accomplished in composing Qauls, it is difficult to sustain Faqueerullah's opinion that Amir Khusrau was the originator of this style, in view of the fact that Qaul has been derived from Qawwali, which was already in existence long before the time of Amir Khusrau, as stated earlier.

In the beginning of sixteenth century, compositions like Qaul have been described in the Sanskrit books also, which proves that Qaul was very much in vogue during that time. Luxmi Narayan, the court scholar of Maharaj Krishna Dev Rai, has described Qaul and Ghazal in his book entitled Sangeet Suryodaya. This was the period when Raja Mansingh of Gwalior and his court musicians were preparing the foundations of Dhruvapad style. Since then Qaul has been a vibrant and fairly popular style of music, and even today some singers of Qaul can be found among the elder generation of musicians. As stated earlier Qaul has been mentioned in most of the manuscripts written during the seventeenth and eighteenth centuries. The most detailed description of this style can be found in Raag Darpan and Tohfat-ul-Hind. Following are two

1. Raag Darpan, p. 45-46.

examples of Qaul :[1]

(1) क़ौल-राग ग़नम ग़नम

स्थाई

मन कुन्तो मौला फ़ा अली मौला
दा रा ति ले दिर दानी

अन्तरा

हम तुम ता ना ना ना ना ना ना ना ना ना ले
या ला ली या ला ली या ला ले
या ला ला या ला ला या ला ला रे

(२) क़ौल-राग चमनी बिलावल

सलाम अल्ला मन रानी जानिब रूए रफतम
अन्तू माने दा नी दानी दि या आहे तहे दा नी

अन्तरा

दिर तिले ल ला रे, दिर तिले ता ना ना दिर ताला
ले तना तिले औ दे नी ते नी ले दा नी
दिर तूम दा रा ती ले दिर तीले तोम त ना ती ला
रे तो म ता तीले तीले दा नी
इलाही आहे अलैकुम शाहे मा बका मन दा नी हबाब

In Risala-e-Zikre Mughannian-e-Hindustan, it has been stated that Qaul was mostly composed in Ek-Taal, Teen-Taal and Chaar-Taal.[2]

Qalbana

Qalbana is similar to Qaul. It is composed with Arabic and Hindi words. The difference between Qaul and Qalbana is that whereas in Qaul there are Arabic words with Tarana syllables, in Qalbana there are Hinidi words and Tarana syllables along with the Arabic compositions. But the major difference between these two styles is that Qaul is composed in only one Taal, while in Qalbana Stet the Taals keep changing in the same composition.[3] An example of Qalbana is given below :[4]

1. Ustad Chand Khan : Mousiqui Hazrat Amir Khusrau ; p. 265.
2. Inayat Khan Rasikh : Risala-e-Zikre-Mughannian-e-Hindustan, p. 14.
3. Mohammad Naqi Khan : Hazrat Amir Khusrau ; p. 199.
4. Hakim Mohammad Karam Imam : Madanul-Mousiqi ; Hindustani Press, Lucknow, 1925.

कलबाना—राग नाथ
ताल सवारी
स्थाई
लकद सदक कौला ताला भेजो दरूद सलाम
अन्तरा
अमीर खुसरो बलि-बलि जावे
हज़रत निज़ामुद्दीन के दरबार गावे कलबाना

It has been noted from the books and manuscripts that like Qaul, it was also a popular style in the seventeenth and eighteenth centuries. It is possible that this form was popularized by the Sufis and saints of the later medieval period, who preferred to use the language of the common man and who, therefore, utilized the Hindi language along with Arabic and Persian language in their compositions. Even today whatever such compositions are traceable, are based on mystic and religious thoughts and feelings. Sometimes the Qawwals sing Qalbana in between their Qawwali performance on the Durgahs of Sufi saints.

It is evident from the descriptions of Qalbana in the books that this must have been a very difficult style in performance, because the Taals in it changed with every Tuk (part) of the song. Unless the Tabla accompanist is fully familiar with the composition and the points at which the Taals are to be changed in it, he would not be able to give a proper accompaniment to the singer. In view of the number of the variations in the Taals in this style of music, some people call it Taal-Sagar.[1]

Naqsh-Gul

Naqsh Gul was a form of musical composition in which Persian words were used. A song which consisted of only one line in Persian language was called Naqsh, and the composition which contained a Persian Rubai was called Naqsh-Gul. In these songs there is description of the beautiful scenes of gardens and flowers in Persian language. They were sung in the Raags of Basant Ritu. It was based on only two parts : Sthayi and Antara. According to Faqueerullah (the author of

1. Ustad Chand Khan : Mcusiqui Hazrat Amir Khusrau; p. 245.

Raag Darpan) Naqsh could also be composed in prose which did not have Ta, Na, Ta, Li, etc. (syllables of Tarana). This form was innovated to match the Hindustani Geet, namely, Man, which was an earlier form of music.[1] Following is an example of Naqsh-Gul :[2]

नक़्श राग बागेरू ताल· तिताला

स्थाई

दिलमन दिलमन दिलमन ईं आवारा दिलमन पारा पारा दिलमन
ईं बेचारा दिलमन, दिलमन दिलमन दिलमन ईं दीवाना दिलमन
आशिक़ जाना दिलमन ईं परवाना दिलमन

अन्तरा

खुसरो दर इश्क़ ख़राब हम चू माही बसराब
सूए मन बेश ताब ईं दीवाना दिलमन

Nigar

This style of music was also based on Persian poetry. According to Faqueerullah, these types of compositions were innovated on the pattern of an older form of Hindustani music named Svaradrutni. It contains a Persian couplet or Rubai. In case of couplet, one line constitutes the Sthayi, and the other line makes the Antara, while in case of Rubai the first couplet becomes the Sthayi and the second couplet is sung as Antara. There is very little difference between Nigar and Naqsh-Gul. The only noticeable difference is that in Nigar there is description of the rainy season, while in Naqsh-Gul there is description of spring. Nigar is sung mostly in the Raags of Malhar Ang.

Baseet

It was originated on the lines of earlier form Chhand.[3] A number of Raags were utilized in such compositions. Usually it consisted of four parts and each part was composed in a different Raag.

Sohela

This style refers to the songs which are sung on the occasion of marriage. These are sung in the style of Khayal, and even the Raags in which these are composed are similar to the Raags of Khayal. Sohelas are composed in shorter Taals, like

1. Faqueerullah : Raag Darpan ; p. 49.
2. Ustad Chand Khan : Mousiqi Hazrat Amir Khusrau : p. 342.
3. Faqueerullah : Raag Darpan ; p. 49.

Jhaptal and Soolfakhta.[1] It contains one Sthayi and two or more Antaras. Following is an example of Sohelas which are heard even today among the older generation of singers :[2]

राग खमाजी बिलावल

ताल कव्वाली

स्थाई

अजमेरी बनड़े सौत काहे तुम पर वारी-वारी

अन्तरा

मेरे ख्वाजा की उंची अटरिया चढ़ा न उतरा जाये

मेरे ख्वाजा से यूं जा कहियो बैंयां पकड़ ले जाये

अजमेरी बनड़े सौत काहे तुम पर वारी वारी

अन्तरा

खुसरो तेरे बल बल जाये निज़ामुद्दीन बलिहारी

कुतुब नगर की गलियां छानी दूल्हा है सरदारी

अजमेरी बनड़े सौत काहे तुम पर वारी-वारी

Trivat

It is a composition based on two to four verses. In this style the syllables of Pakhawaj are composed and sung in different Raags.[3]

Kaane

This style was popular in the province of Sind. It was believed to be utilized for Tona (sorcery) and magic.[4] It consisted of romantic and love songs.

Zakri

It was based on few verses and phrases. It was popular among the Muslims of Gujarat and the songs in it contained idealistic and philosophical notions.[5] According to Raag Darpan the number of verses were not fixed, and each verse was completed with a Baran.[6] Qazi Mohammad Gujrati was the originator of this style. The songs in this form contained the themes of love, passion and sometimes death also. Following is an example of Zakri which was composed by Syed Shah

1. Ibid., p. 243.
2. Ustad Chand Khan : Mousiqi Hazrat Amir Khusrau, p. 371.
3. Faqueerullah : Raag Darpan ; p. 49.
4. Ibid, p. 50.
5. See Tohfat-ul-Hind, edited by N.H. Ansari.
6. The word Baran here may perhaps be synonymous with Varna,

Hashim Al-Ulvi (A.D. 1649):

कहियो हो चक मेरे पीव, मीत दिनन का उलझा जीव ।
बादर कूट घटा घिर आवे, तिल धारनं भीजी खड़ी खिजाये ।
मोर चिकारे है बन माती, पशु पंखी सब तेरे राती ।
कई कई भांतू भाव दिखाते कहियो हो चक मेरे पीव ।
मीत दिनन का उलझा जीव ।
बीर बहूटी रंग रत मेरे मोर पिया घर आव सवेरे ।
कहियो हो चक मेरे पीव ।
मीत दिनन का उलझा जीव ।
नैन हमारे निसदिन रोवे, मीत बना कहो क्यों जनम खोवे ।
हाशिम जी सुख होवे, तब मुख मीता जोवे ।
कहियो हो चक मेरे पीव ।
मीत दिनन का उलझा जीव ।[1]

Lachari

These songs were sung in the region of Tirhut (a region in Bihar). Usually the songs in this style revolved around the theme of love. Lachari is still sung in some of the areas of Bihar and east U.P. at present also.

Gujri

This was sung in Gujarat. It contained description of wars and adoration of Kings.

Kadhka

It has been described by some writers as Katurkha also. It was composed of four or eight verses in Rajasthani language. Each part of it consisted of two verses. The songs in it contained accounts of the description of wars and courageous persons. Sometimes the bravery of the Kings was also praised in these songs. It was called Kadhka because it was based on a few Kadhis. Kadhi refers to a short verse or Tuk.[2] According to Ain-e-Akbari, in earlier stages Dhadis (a section of musicians) used to sing Kadhka, but gradually these songs were being sung by a section of persons namely Kadhket.

Sadra

It was also sung in the style of Khayal. According to Tohfat-ul-Hind, Sadra was always composed in the language of

1. Brihaspati : Musalman Aur Bhartiya Sangeet. p. 110,
2. Tohfat-ul-Hind

Mathura or Braj Bhasha. It contained four, six or eight verses. According to Raag Darpan the songs in it described the warriors, their courage and personality.[1] It is noteworthy that the present style of Sadra is quite different from its earlier version. These days Sadra refers to the songs sung in Jhaptal.

Mangal Ishtak and Jaitshri

These songs were sung for rejoicing on the occasions of marriage.[2]

Chhand

Regarding this style Faqueerullah has stated that it was popular around Lahore. Zakaria Multani had referred to it as Chind also, and he had introduced many improvisations in this style. A few verses in it are devoted to the praise of God.[3]

Maankal

It was composed in all Desi languages, but it was more popular in Jaunpur. The number of verses in it was not fixed. Each verse was repeated twice. Mostly love tales were described in these types of songs.[4]

Bigad

It was composed in the language of Rajputana. The songs in this style described the courage and valour of the warriors, and the stories of the battles fought by them.

Baar

Some people called it Baad also. This was sung in the Charni language. Charan referred to the nomadic tribes of Banjaras and the Jaat community. These songs were sung only by the Dhadhis. There was no restriction on the number of verses in its compositions. In these compositions there used to be detailed descriptions of battles. It was sung by a team of at least two persons in which the first two verses were recited by the leader of the team, and the third verse was recited by the group of followers.[5]

Chutkula

It consisted of two verses, without Qafia (the final conso-

1. Faqueerullah : Raag Darpan, p. 52.
2. Ibid, p. 52.
3. Ibid., p. 52.
4. Ibid., p. 53.
5. Faqueerullah : Raag Darpan, p. 53.

nant on which the rhythm of the poem rests). It was based on songs in praise of love and affection and when the songs of Chutkula described the stories of wars it was called Sadhar Chutkula. The originator of this style was Sultan Hussain Sharqui, the King of Jaunpur.[1] It consisted of four parts, namely : Sthayi, Antara, Sanchari, and Abhog. It was sung in twelve Taals in a sequence. In some books it has been described as Chatkala.

Farsi

It contained Persian couplets or Tarana syllables and it was composed in Ek-Taal.

Bal-Leela

These songs were sung on the occasion of child birth. Like Khayal it also contained two verses.

Vishnu Pad

These songs were sung in praise of Lord Krishna. They contained four to eight verses.

Karsh and Bagdhar

In addition to the abovementioned styles there is mention of Karsh and Bagdhar also. The description of these songs is not very clear. However, the overall impression one gets on reading these descriptions is that these were the songs of Desi style.

Tappa

Tappa has not been described in most of the books of seventeenth and eighteenth centuries. There is only a short description of it in Raag Darpan. According to Raag Darpan, "It is composed in two, four or more verses. It contains pairs of two verses separately. There is description of sorcery and death in these songs".[2]

It is interesting to note that the contemporary Tappa songs are quite different compared to the description of Tappas of Raag Darpan. Evidently, this style has undergone considerable change during the intervening period, as the theme of Tappa songs is mostly romantic at the present time.

Tappa is believed to have been innovated by Shori Mian. It has, however, not yet been established clearly by the writers

1. Ibid., p. 40.
2. Faqueerullah : Raag Darpan, p. 53.

and scholars of music whether Shori was a man or a woman's name. Mostly the writers uphold the view that Ghulam Nabi Shori was a man who innovated this style. But few writers have given a different viewpoint by stating that Shori was the name of a woman who was Ghulam Nabi's wife.[1]

An important point to be noted here is that the general belief regarding the innovation of Tappa by Shori Mian would mean that this style started in the year 1810 A.D. which was the period when Shori Mian was living in Lucknow. But the description of Tappa in Raag Darpan, as stated above, indicates that such a style existed earlier in the seventeenth century also. As mentioned earlier, the Tappas today contain themes of love and romance, as compared to the theme of sorcery and death as described in Raag Darpan. It is, therefore possible that Shori gave it a new shape and content which is prevalent today. It is interesting to note that in Madan-ul-Mousiqi this term has been written as Dappa.[2]

Thumri

It is strange and surprising to note that in the various manuscripts and books written during the seventeenth and eighteenth centuries examined in connection with this study, there was no mention of Thumri as a style of music. Interestingly, there is mention of Thumri in some of these books and manuscripts as a Raag. In Tohfat-ul-Hind, Thumri has been described as the Ragini of Shri Raag according to Bharat Mat. While discussing the Raag the author has said : "the Raag named Thumri is very popular in the eastern part of the country".

In Raag Darpan, Thumri has been described as a Dhun of Raag Barwa. Thumri has also been mentioned as a Raag in Shri Radha Govind Sangitsar which was written during the eighteenth century. In Usulun-Naghmat-e-Asifi, it has been classified as a Ragini of Shri Raag. Captain Willard described Thumri as a Raag. The description indicates that it was a Raag which was composed by combining Shankarabharana and

1. Hazrat Amir Khusrau Ka Ilm-e-Mousiqi Aur Doosre Maqalat ; p. 26.

2. Hakim Mohd, Karaam Imam ; Madan-ul-Mausiqui, p, 167, Hindustani Press Lucknow, 1925.

Maru Raag.[1]

The above mentioned account of Thumri in the literature belonging to the seventeenth and eighteenth centuries proves the point that Thumri had not developed as an independent form of music until that period. Even if it might have existed at that time, it could not have been a popular style.

The most widely current theory about Thumri attributes the origin of this musical style to the royal court of Oudh, especially that of Nawab Wajid Ali Shah.[2] According to some authors the origin of Thumri is connected with Bhajan and it was developed in the Vaishnavite temples. According to general belief, Shori Mian has been described as the originator of this style. This point of view does not seem to be supported by any dependable evidence. It is possible that Shori was associated with Thumri, because Shori Mian belonged to Lucknow and Thumri was a very popular style during that period.

A detailed study of the origin, development and its present form indicates that Thumri is a North Indian Desi form of singing which was utilized by the female dancers to accompany their expressive dancing forms. Later, Thumri developed into a separate and independent style of music. However, the nature and form in which it might have existed during the seventeenth and eighteenth centuries is a mystery.

Dhamal

Dhamal or Dhamali is sung in Dhamar Taal. It is also called Hori Geet. In folk music it is a group song which is sung in small teams. Pakhawaj is used for the accompaniment in these songs. A special characteristic of this song is the description of Krishna and Gopis, playing Hori.[3] Some writers believe that earlier Dhamal was sung in the musical sittings of the Sufi Saints who used to hold hands and dance together in ecstasy.[4]

1. Bhatkhande Sangeet Shastra Part-I, p. 62.
2. Sharma, Premlata : 'Thumri', Indian Music Journal, Oct.-Nov., 1960.
3. Brihaspati : 'Dhamar Gayaki, Ek Rangarang Parampara', Sangeet, Apr., 1968.
4. Ustad Chand Khan : Mousiqi Hazrat Amir Khusrau, p. 247.

Earlier Dhamal was sung in the temples but during the medieval times it became a part of the court music. An example of such Dhamal in the Yaman Raag in which the name of Emperor Akbar has been mentioned is given below :

होरी खेलई बनेगी रूसें अब न वनैगी
मोरो कहो तू मानि नवेली ज वा रंग में सनैगी
कैई बेरि आई गई तू, नाहीं मानत
ऊंची करि ठोड़ि मौंहे तनैगी
साहि जलालदीन फगुआ दीजै, आपुते-आप मनैगी[1]

In Nadirat-e-Shahi, which was compiled during the time of Shah Alam there are several examples of such beautiful Dhamars. Niyamat Khan Sadarang, a court musician during Mohammad Shah Rangila's time, has composed several songs in this style. For example :

अब तो महम्मद साहि पिय घर आये
चहल पहल फागुन की देखौ जित जित सदारंग बरसाए
चैन से गाओ आओ रहसि रहसि
कहि लाखनि लाखनि पाए
इक होरी दूजे नहाए रंग सो यह गुन गिने न जाते गिनाये[2]

Some Unknown Forms of Hindustani Music

In addition to the styles and forms of Hindustani Music discussed above, the writers of later medieval period have mentioned about the Margi-Sangeet also. According to these writers, the Margi-Sangeet had begun to decline and was nearly extinct by their time. While describing Margi Sangeet, Faqueerullah says : "Margi refers to the songs which are sung by the gods. It is difficult to describe such songs. It is rarely heard in North India. But in South India, where Desi Raags are not popular, it is likely that the music of that part might be similar to the Margi Sangeet. However, some musicians of the South who came and met me have informed me that the singers of Margi Sangeet have become rare in the

1. Brihaspati : 'Dhamar Gayaki, Ek Rangarang Parampara, Sangeet, Apr., 1968.
2. Ibid.
3. Faqueerullah : Raag Darpan; p. 37.

South also. Even those who are familiar with Margi Sangeet have started singing Desi Sangeet".[1]

In all the major manuscripts discussed in this study, we find a mention of some unknown forms and styles of music after the mention of Margi Sangeet. Out of several such forms, three forms of music mentioned in these books have not been mentioned anywhere in the contemporary literature. These forms, therefore, deserve our special attention due to their uniqueness.

According to the authors of these manuscripts, Geet is a form of music which is sung in adoration of kings, gods, and goddesses, and it is of three types :

(1) Suraj Prakash
(2) Chandra Prakash
(3) Siratyu Bhadra (probably Shruti Bhadra)

Suraj Prakash

It was composed in praise of kings and gods.[2] It contained Chhand, Svar and Tanas also. Its verbal text was of a high standard. Both the Sargam and Akar were utilized in this style of music. The origin of this style was believed to be associated with Brahma and Samved.[3] Twelve Kalas have been identified as related to this type of song.

Chandra Prakash

The description of Chandra Prakash is vague. It has been stated that Chandra Prakash was sung and completed in one Prahar (three-hour duration or a quarter of a day). Sixteen Kalas were recognized as associated with this song. Chandra Prakash and Suraj Prakash can be structured with the help of the Kalas of the sun and moon.

Sur Bhadra or Shruti Bhadra

This contains numerous verses, and the Taal in it is repeated four times.

The description of above mentioned styles is not very clear. These have been mentioned in Raag Darpan and Usulun-Naghmat-e-Asifi, but not in Tohfat-ul-Hind. It is also difficult to trace these styles in the Sanskrit writings of that period.

1. Faqueerullah : **Raag Darpan**; p. 37.
2. Faqueerullah : **Raag Darpan** ; p. 37.
2. Reza, Ghulam : **Usulun-Naghmat-e-Asifi.**

A detailed study of these styles might give some clues regarding the Margi Sangeet.

It is interesting to note that in Sangeet Makrand, the terms Suryauns and Chandrauns are traceable. These terms are mentioned in the context of categorization of Raags. Although it is very difficult to say how far these terms relate to Suraj Prakash and Chandra Prakash, because these terms are described in Persian works as the styles of singing, yet a further detailed study of Sanskrit texts may give some more clues regarding these terms.

Raag Kudam

Regarding this style Faqueerullah states : "The theme of songs in this style is the description of the elegance and adornment of Nayika. A number of Raags and Taals are included in its compositions. It is almost an extinct form of music in the north, but some people still sing it in the south".[1] It could be composed on few verses.[2] In Sangeet Ratnakar, a type of Prabandha called Raag Kadamb has been mentioned, the description of which is somewhat similar to Raag Kudam.

Snr Adrutni

This style of songs has been mentioned in some of the Persian manuscripts, but no details have been given. The author of Madan-ul-Mousiqi has given a short description of Sur Adrutni. According to him, these types of songs were based on Svar, Taal, and a few meaningless syllables.[3]

Dhva

This style has not been described clearly. In some manuscripts it has been mentioned as Dhruva also. According to Tohfat-ul-Hind, Dhva consisted of four Khands (parts). But no further detailed description of this style has been given in the literature of the seventeenth and eighteenth centuries. However, in Ghuniyat-ul-Munya, which was written during the fourteenth century, the following description of Dhva has been given :

"Dhva is one of the most important varieties of Salag-

1. Faqueerullah : Raag Darpan; p. 37.
2. Hakim Mohammad Karam Imam : Madan-ul-oMusiqi, p.164.
3. Hakim Mohammad Karam Imam : Madan-ul-Mousqi, p. 164.

Suda. Without Dhva, Salag-Suda remains dull and incomplete like a woman without a man. Dhva is sung in six stages".[1] Further sixteen varieties of Dhva have been described. The names of sixteen Dhvas, and the Taals and Rasas associated with them have been described as given below :

Dhva	Taal	Ras
1. Jayant	Adital	Sringar
2. Shekhar	Ni-Saru	Veer
3. Uchchah (Utsah)	Pramath	Hasya
4. Madhur	Haililak	Karuna
5. Nirmal	Krida	Shringar
6. Kuntal	Laghu-Shikhar	Adbhut
7. Kamal	Jhampa	Vipralambh
8. Charu	Ni-Saru	Vir
9. Nandan	Iktali	Vir Sringar
10. Chandrasekhar	Pramath	Vir-Hasya-Sringar
11. Kamod	Pramath	Sringar
12. Vijaya	Dwitiya	Hasya
13. Kandarp	Adital	Hasya, Sringar Karuna
14. Jai Mangal	Krida	Sringar-Vir
15. Tilak	Iktali	Vir-Sringar
16. Lalit	Pramath	Sringar

It is interesting to note that in Sangeet Ratnakar of Sarangdev, there is a description of a variety of Prabandha, which totally resembles with the description of Dhva as given in Ghunyat' ul-Munya and Tohfat-ul-Hind.

The above description clearly proves that Dhva as mentioned in the literature of the seventeenth and eighteenth centuries refers to no other form, but to Dhruva Prabandha as given in Sangeet Ratnakar. Probably this style was popular earlier but declined and almost disappeared from the scene by the end of the eighteenth century. The following description of Dhruva Prabandha as quoted from Sangeet Ratnakar is worthy of note for comparison with the description of Dhva in Ghunyat-ul-Munya :

1. Ghunyat-ul-Munya, edited by Shahab Sarmadee, Asia Publishing House, Bombay, 1978; p. 33-34.

एकधातुर्द्विखण्डः स्याद्यत्रोद्ग्राहस्ततः परम्
किंचिदुच्चं भवेत् खण्डं द्विरभ्यस्तमिदं त्रयम
ततो द्विखण्ड आभोगस्तस्य स्यात् खण्डमादिमम्
एकधातु द्विखण्डं च खण्डमुच्चतरं परम्
स्तुत्यनामाँकितश्चासौ क्वचिदुच्चकखण्डकः
उद्ग्राहस्याद्यखण्डे च न्यासः स ध्रुवको भवेत्
एकादशाक्षरात् खण्डादेकैकाक्षरवर्धितैः
खण्डे ध्रवाः षोडश स्युः षडविंशत्यक्षरावधि
जयन्तशेखरोत्साहास्तो मधुरनिर्मलौ
कुन्तलः कामलश्चारो नन्दनश्चन्द्रशेखरः
कामोदो विजयाख्यश्च कंदर्पजयमंगलौ
तिलको ललितश्चेति संक्षारचेषा क्रमादिमाः

Similary, three other styles, Jhoomra, Matha, and Parmath, have been mentioned in the literature of the period without giving much details of these styles. Further, it has been stated that they belonged to the earlier period and were on the verge of extinction at that time. A closer study of these styles reveals that they were similar to the Jhombad Prabandha, Matth Prabandha, and Pramath Prabandha respectively, as described in Sangeet Ratnakar.

The foregoing description and analysis of various forms and styles of music prevalent during the seventeenth and eighteenth centuries, and those styles which have been mentioned in the literature during that period, have enabled us to understand the emergence, zenith and decline of some of the well known as well as obscure and extinct musical forms of Hindustani music. We have explored the origin, development, modifications, innovations, and transformations in famous contemporary styles like Dhruvapad, Khayal, Tarana, and Qawwali particularly during the period under study. The study explodes many myths and commonly held notions about the origin of these forms. We have also discovered some unknown and unique forms which were practised during that period, or were practised earlier and were phasing out with the passage of time. It is evident from this analysis that the seventeenth and eighteenth centuries were a period of considerable enrichment, blending and innovation in Hindustani Music.

In the next section we shall describe the musicians of this period, their art and skills, the social and cultural milieu in which they performed, their musical instruments, their unique styles, and their peculiarities as described in literature.

SECTION C

Musicians of the Seventeenth and Eighteenth Centuries

In the first two Sections of this study the major manuscripts and the development of various forms and styles of music have been discussed. In this Section we will examine the descriptions of musicians belonging to the seventeenth and eighteenth centuries about whom written records are available. Thus, this Section will complete the three parts of the framework on which the study has been based. A survey of the literature in Hindustani Music shows that relatively little importance has been given to the biographies of musicians and the information regarding their talents and artistic achievements. It may be emphasized that this is a very important source of information about the state of art and the special features of music during a particular period. Unfortunately, very little has been written about the musicians by the musicologists, while the historians could not record in detail the technicalities and subtleties of the art of such musicians. Inspite of these limitations, whatever information is available from the manuscripts and the historical books pertaining to the seventeenth and eighteenth centuries has been presented in this Section.

CHAPTER VIII

Names and Description of Musicians and their Musical Styles

SINCE the ancient times the musicians have been classified into various categories, as is evident from the Shastric writings. In the earlier chapters it has been stated that the musicians were grouped together on the basis of the quality of their voice and their skilfulness in performance. On the basis of the above mentioned two factors, different names were given to the musicians which have already been described in the previous chapters. In most of the ancient Sanskrit works musicians were categorized into three types : (1) Uttam; (2) Madhyam; (3) Nikrisht.

Later, the classification was based mainly on the competence and knowledge of the musiciains, and they were categorized as follows :

(1) Gandharva (2) Gunkar (3) Pundit (4) Nayak (5) Gayak.

It may be noted here that the basis of classification of musicians underwent a change during the medieval period. In addition to the above mentioned classical approaches, the authors during this period included additional factors for classifying the musicians, such as the type of songs sung by them, and the type of community or caste to which they belonged.

In Madan-ul-Mousiqi, Hakim Mohammad Karam Imam has described the musicians of medieval period according to the following categories : (1) Gandharva; (2) Gunkar; (3) Pundit: (4) Nayak; (5) Gayak (6) Kalawant; (7) Qawwal, (8) Dhadhi.

From the above mentioned categories, the last three (Kalawant, Qawwal and Dhadhi) deserve special attention, because these categories have been frequently mentioned in the Persian and Urdu literature of the seventeenth and eighteenth centuries. Following is a brief description of these categories :

Kalawant : The musicians who sang Dhruvapad or Trivat and songs of similar variety were known as Kalawants.[1]

Qawwal : The musicians who were capable of singing Khayal, Qaul, Qalbana, Naqsh-Gul and Tarana were known as Qawwals.[2]

Dhadhi : This category of musicians was in existence much before the Kalawants and Qawwals. Earlier, they used to sing Kadhka (the war songs), and it is said that they were converts from Hinduism to Islam.[3] According to Ain-e-Akbari, the Dhadhis sang songs in praise of the courage and valour of the brave soldiers and they added glamour to the battle field. Such war songs were known as Sindhu in Marwar, which was a particular type of Raag, and it was sung by the Dhadhis in the front ranks of the army.[4]

The Dhadhis and Dholis belonged to the same broad category of musicians. But the difference between the two was that Dholis used to play Dhols, while the Dhadhis played Sarangi or Rebab. Dhadhis belonged to both the Hindu and Muslim communities. The Muslim Dhadhis were known as Malanoor.[5]

Two more categories of musicians have been mentioned in Raag Darpan. These are : Samit and Tatar. The author has not given details about these categories of musicians.

According to Ain-e-Akbari and other relevant sources, following are the names of the prominent musicians belonging to Akbar's court, and most of them were living and performing

1. Karam Imam, Hakim Mohammad : Madan-ul-Mousiqi, p. 125.
2. Karam Imam, Hakim Mohammad ; Madan-ul-Mousiqi, p. 125.
3. Ibid., p. 125.
4. Nahata, Agarchand : Rajasthan Ki Gaane Bajaane Waali Qaumen aur Dhadhi, Sangeet, Oct., 1961.
5. **Ibid.**

in the early seventeenth century also :

(1) Baba Ramdas Bairagi (2) Tansen (3) Subhan Khan Gwaliori (4) Mian Chand (5) Surgyan Khan (6) Vichitra Khan (brother of Subhan Khan) (7) Mohammad Khan (8) Veer Mandal Khan of Gwalior (Surmandal player) (9) Ustad Yusuf Harvi (Tamboora player) (10) Qasim (inventor of an instrument similar to Rebab) (11) Tara Beg (Qabz player) (12) Sultan Hafiz Hussain (13) Baz Bahadur (14) Shahab Khan Gwaliori (15) Daood Dhadhi (16) Sarood Khan (17) Mian Lal Gwaliori (18) Tan Tarang Khan (son of Tansen) (19)Mulla Ishaq (20) Ustad Dost (Nae, a type of a flute player) (21) Baharam Quli (Ghichki player) (22) Sultan Hashim (Tamboor-player) (23) Ustad Shah Mohammad (24) Ustad Mohammad Amin (Tamboor player) (25) Nayak Charju Gwaliori (26) Prabeen Khan (Been player) (27) Soordas (son of Ramdas) (28) Chand Khan Gwaliori (29) Rangsen of Agra (30) Sheikh Dawan (Karna player) (31) Rahmatulla (brother of Mulla Ishaq) (32) Mir Sayed Ali (Ghichki player) (33) Hafiz Khwaja Ali (34) Mir Abdullah (Qanoon player) (35) Peerzada (36) Ustad Mohammad Hussain (Tamboor player).

According to Tuzuk-e-Jahangiri, Shahjahan Nama, Risaala-e-Zikr-e-Mughannian-e-Hindustan and other relevant sources, following is a list of famous musicians who belonged to seventeenth and eighteenth centuries : (1) Vilas Khan (2) Chhattar Khan (3) Khurram Daad (4) Makkhoo (5) Hamjan (6) Shauqui (7) Ustad Mohammad (8) Lal Khan Kalawant (9) Khushhal Khan—Bisram (10) Rang Khan Kalawant (11) Kishan Khan Kalawant (12) Jagannath Kavirai (13) Sheikh Sher Mohammad and Sheikh Kabir (14) Sheikh Moinuddin (15) Zulqarn (16) Budh Singh (17) Mirza Aaquil (18) Misri Khan Dhadhi (19) Mir Salesh Qawwal (20) Kun Sen (21) Hasan Khan Nauhar (22) Sheikh Kamal (23) Bakht Khan Gujrati (24) Basanti Kalawanti (25) Ghulam Mohiuddin (26) Kun Khan Kalawant (27) Vali Dhadhi (28) Salim Chand Dagar (29) Sheikh Sadullah Lahori (30) Mohammad Baaqui (31) Pooja (32) Bazeed Khan Nauchhawari (33) Roora Qawwal (34) Kabir Qawwal (35) Tulsi Ram (36) Dharamdas (37) Rahimdad Dhadhi (38) Idul Singh (39) Mir Ammad (40)

Hamir Sen—Subal Sen (41) Sayed Khan Nauhar (42) Sayed Tayyab (43) Sunder Ghan (44) Madhu Nayak.

Out of the above mentioned two lists of the names of the musicians, a description of those musicians has been given below, about whom some details could be obtained from the available literature :

Baz-Bahadur

He was the Governor of Malwa. During his time Malwa had become a centre of music and musicians. He was himself an accomplished musician. A novel style of music was innovated by him which was known as Baz Khani. His wife Rupmati was very knowledgeable about music. She committed suicide in the 1560 A.D. after the defeat of her husband by emperor Akbar.[1]

Baba Ramdas Bairagi

He was a resident of Gwalior and was a court musician of Akbar and Jahangir. He had a close relationship with Abdur-Rahim-Khan-e-Khana. His singing often used to move Khan-e-Khana to tears. Ramdas has also been described as the teacher of Tansen. His son Surdas was a distinguished musician of his time.[2]

Nayak Dhondhu

Nayak Dhondhu was a disciple of Baba Ramdas. Ramdas and Dhondhu were very famous for singing of Dhruvapad and Vishnupad. The Dhruvapads and Vishnupads composed by them were very well known during their time. They used to live in Burz Desh (Mathura).[3]

Tansen

Tansen's birth is ascribed to the prayer and blessings of Sheikh Mohammad Ghaus of Gwalior. When he was five years old, his father brought him to Sheikh. Since then Tansen lived with Sheikh Mohammad Ghaus. It is believed that Tansen was deeply impressed by the compositions of

1. Arshi, I.A. : 'Hindustan Ke Chand Mashhoor Mousiqaar'; Aaaj Kal, Aug., 1956.

2. Ibid.

3. Rasikh, I.K. (ed) : Risala-e-Zikr-e-Mughannian-e-Hindustan, p. 19.

Nayak Bakhshoo and he decided to learn the art of music.[1] After the death of Mohammad Ghaus he went to Daulat Khan, the son of Sher Shah. When Sher Shah expired, he moved over to Raja Ram Chandra Baghela of Rewa, where he was highly honoured. When emperor Akbar came to know about Tansen's fame, he asked the Raja to send Tansen over to his court. His novel style of singing pleased the emperor and Tansen lived at Akbar's court with great honour and respect. Tansen was included among the nine gems of Akbar's court. He died in the year 1580 A,D.[2]

According to Ain-e-Akbari, neither a musician like Tansen existed during the last one thousand years, nor will any such musician be born in the next thousand years. He introduced a number of new Raags[3] such as : (1) Darbari Kanhra—a combination of Kanhra, Malhar and Kalyan (2) Jogiya—a combination of Asavari and Dev Gandhar (3) Mian Ki Malhar—a combination of Malhar and Kanhra, (4) Mian Ki Todi (5) Mian Ki Sarang.

It is surprising to note that inspite of the enormous popularity and distinction of his art, he was not given the title of Nayak. Instead, he has been categorized as a Pundit. According to some writers he was categorized as Gandharva. Probably the reason for this anomaly was as stated in Raag Darpan, that most of the musicians in Akbar's court were merely performing artistes and were not recognised as knowledgeable in the Shastras of music.[4] According to Hakim Mohammad Karam Imam, the author of Madan-ul-Mousiqi, earlier the art of music was considered to be a source of spiritual satisfaction, but Tansen made it a means of livelihood, and he performed to please the emperor for his material gains. That is why Tansen could not be called a Nayak.

Chand Khan and Suraj Khan

These two brothers belonged to Gwalior. Both of them were regarded great musicians of Akbar's court. They were

1. Arshi, I.A.; op. cit.
2. See Ain-e-Akbari, Akbarnama and Khulasat-ul-Aish Alamshahi.
3. Arshi, I.A. ; op. cit.
4. Faqueerullah : Raag Darpan; p. 89.

often called Ravi and Shashi. They were given the status of Gandharvas. The rigour for their training can be understood by the fact that they trained their son one Sthayi of a song for twelve years.[1]

Nayak Charju

Nayak Charju was a resident of Gwalior and a court musician of Akbar. He was considered to be a Nayak on the basis of his knowledge and skill. It is said that he was highly knowledgeable about two out of the four Matas (Bharat, Hanuman, Kallinath, Someshvar). His son Prabeen Khan was also Akbar's court musician and was an accomplished Been player.[2]

Mian Lal

He hailed from Gwalior and was one of the few musicians who were close to Akbar. Since childhood he joined Akbar's court and was brought up and trained there. At the age of twenty, he died in the year 1608 A.D. He had a favourite slave girl, from whose hands he used to take opium regularly. After the death of Mian, she also committed suicide by taking opium.[3]

Tan Tarang Khan

He was one of the three sons of Tansen and was the most famous among his brothers. His name has been included among the distinguished singers of Akbar's court in Ain-e-Akbari. He was given the rank of Gandharva.[4]

Bilas Khan and Surat Sen

These two were also sons of Tansen. The variety of Todi known as Bilaskhani Todi was innovoted by Bilas Khan.[5]

Mirza Aaquil

He was the son of Baqar Khan and disciple of Tansen. He had also attained the status of Gandharva.[6]

Sujan Khan

His real title was Surjan Khan, and over a period of

1. Arshi, I.A. ; op. cit.
2. Ibid.
3. Arshi, I.A. ; op. cit.
4. Ibid.
5. Ibid.
6. Ibid.

time he began to be called Sujan Khan. He was resident of Gwalior. He had also visited the holy Mecca and Medina and it is said that he gave musical performance in Medina and sang Raag Dipak at the insistence of his admirers. His brother was also Akbar's court musician.[1]

Lal Khan Kalawant

Lal Khan was the son-in-law of Tansen's son Bilas Khan. He was the most outstanding and honoured musician of the court of Shahjahan. In the year 1637 A.D. Shahjahan bestowed on him the title of Gun Samudra. His style of singing resembled Tansen's singing, which he acquired from the disciples of Tansen. He was unparalleled in Dhruvapad singing. He had four sons who used to accompany him in his performances. He expired in 1654 A.D. at Agra.[2]

Khushhal Khan and Bisram

These two were sons of Lal Khan and maternal grandsons of Bilas Khan. Among his brothers, Khushhal Khan was the best singer and he used to include Shahjahan's name in his compositions.[3] In his book Raag Darpan, Faqueerullah has stated about Khushhal Khan : "He was in Shahjahan's court, and is still alive. He has close contact with emperor Aurangzeb. May God give him a long life as he has no parallel among the Kalawants".[4] Bisram also used to sing like Khushhal Khan. These two were regarded as the best singers of Shahjahan's court. There is a well known story associated with these musicians. It is said that once Aurangzeb wanted Murshid Quli Khan to accompany him. But Murshid Quli Khan was not getting emperor Shahjahan's permission. When Khushhal and Bisram came to know about it, they offered to obtain the signatures for the release of Murshid Quli Khan, if they were given one lakh rupees. Having struck the deal, on the occasion of Nauroze when a large musical gathering was arranged, they sat at a distance of ten yards from the

1. Ibid.
2. Rasikh, Inayat Khan (ed.) : Risala-e-Zikr-e-Mughannian-e-Hindustan p. 13.
3. Brihaspati : Musalman Aur Bhartiya Sangeet, p. 76.
4. Faqueerullah : Raag Darpan, p. 98.

emperor's throne and sang Raag Todi, which was often called Darbari Todi. Shahjahan was very fond of this particular Raag. Khushhal and Bisrm sang a Dhruvapad in this Raag which totally absorbed the emperor. Finding the occasion suitable, Khushhal and Bisram gave a hint to Amir-ul-Umra who placed the document before the emperor, who signed it without looking at it, and thus Aurangzeb's purpose was served. Later, when Shahjahan came to know about this intrigue, he was very angry. Consequently, they were denied the rank which was given to their predecessor Tansen.[1]

Budh Singh

Budh Singh was the son of Ardh Singh, the Raja of Boondi. He could sing several forms of music, particularly Desi Geets. He accompanied prince Muazzam Shah who went to Kabul as Governor during the last days of Shahjahan's rule. Budh Singh was also a patron of several musicians and he used to extend his hospitality to them. He died during the first few years of Shah Alam's period.[2]

Sheikh Sher Mohammad and His Disciple Sheikh Kabir

These two were incomparable Qawwali singers of their time. Both were court musicians of Dara Shikoh. The lady with whom Dara Shikoh was in love was the disciple of these musicians. They also used to visit Shahjahan. Both of them belonged to Akbarabad.[3] Faqueerullah has given some information about Sheikh Sher Mohammad in Raag Darpan. According to him : "Sheikh Sher Mohammad used to sing Chutkula, Dhruvapad, Khayal, Tarana, etc., and there was no particular uniqueness in their singing. When I saw him, he was not very old. He died in Patna at the age of fifty six years.[4]

Sheikh Moinuddin

According to Inayat Khan Rasikh, "Sheikh Moinuddin is

1. Rasikh, I. K. (ed.), : Risala-e-Zikr-e-Mughannian-e-Hindustan; p. 18.
2. Rasikh, I.K (ed), : Risala-e-Zikr-e-Mughannian-e-Hindustan; p. 29.
3. Ibid.
4. Faqueerullah : Raag Darpan, p. 92.

the son of Sher Mohammod and he is still alive. He is an exemplary singer of Khayal, Qaul and Tarana.[1]

Zulqarn

He was often called Zulqarn Firangi. He had composed several Dhruvapads. He was Amir and Faujdar of Sambhar Pargana during the period of Alamgir, and he died there only.[2]

Madhu Nayak

Madhu Nayak was a resident of Bilgram. He had a unique place among the musicians of his time. He was an extremely courteous person with a tremendous sense of humour. He learnt Hindi and Sanskrit languages in Banaras and acquired a high degree of excellence in these languages. At the same time he studied the art of music thoroughly and became a highly knowledgeable scholar in the subject of Nad, Tal and Geet. As a result of his scholastic attainments in music he was regarded as a Nayak of his time. He was fomous for his compositions of Naqsh. The musicians of his time held him in high esteem. He lived with Nawab Kamaluddin Bin Nawab Diler Khan of Shahjahanabad, where he was given great respect. He died in his home in the year 1688 A.D.[3]

In Raag Darpan, Faquerullah has given a description of some well known musicians before his time as well as of the musicians who were living during his time as given below :

Sheikh Bahauddin

He had learnt music in the Deccan. His home town was Jhunjhuna. He always used to wear dresses in green colour. He used to sing Geet, Dhruvapad, Khayal, Tarana, etc. He used to play Rebab and Abhvritti. He designed an instrument which he named Khayal.[4]

Sher Mohammad

This musician has already been described earlier in this chapter.

Jagannath Kaviraj

The title of Jagannath was Kaviraj. It is said that he was a

1. Rasikh, I.K (ed). : Risala-e-Zikr-e-Mughannian-e-Hindustan p. 27.
2. Ibid.
3. Arshi, I.A : op. cit.
4. Faqueerullah : Raag Darpan, p. 91.

musician of the stature of Tansen. Once he composed a Dhruvapad in Raag Nat and sang it before Tansen. On hearing this song Tansen remarked: "After me the musician who deserves my place is Jagannath".[1]

Mian Danoo Dhadhi

He lived like Durveshes and played Saboo with great perfection.

Misri Khan Dhadhi

He was one of the disciples of Vilas Khan. He went to Bengal with Sultan Shuja Khan. His compositions were of good quality and were very popuplar.[2] He was eighty years old when Faqueerullah wrote about him.

Mir Saleh Qawwal

He was a resident of Delhi and was an accomplished singer. He died at the age of nineteen.

Hasan Khan Nauhar

He was a popular singer. But in Faqueerullah's opinion his singing was ordinary. He died at the age of fiftysix.

Gun Sen

His real name was Nayak Afzal and Gun Sen was his pseudonym. He could sing Kavitt very well. He was outstanding in the knowledge of Margi Sangeet among his contemporary musicians. He died at the age of fiftysix in Kashmir. His compositions are reasonably good.[3]

Sheikh Kamaal

He was the disciple of Mian Dhalu, He was in military service and lived with Faqueerullah for some time. He could sing reasonably well.[4]

Bakht Khan Gujrati

He was a Kalawant belonging to Gujrat and was a disciple of Bilas Khan. Faqueerullah states: "Although I have seen him, I have not heard him, but my musician friends spoke highly of his art. He died at the age of fifty six. Basanti Kalawanti, who was his disciple, was a good singer, and I had an opportunity of listening to her".[5]

1. Faqueerullah: Raag Darpan, p. 91.
2. Ibid.
3. Ibid; p. 98.
4. Ibid.
5. Ibid., p. 97.

Rang Khan

He was a Kalawant of high reputation and he was a musician of Shahjahan's court also. In his childhood he had seen the musicians of Akbar's period.[1]

Khushhal Khan

His description has already been given earlier.

Ghulam Mohiuddin

He ceased to be a soldier and became a musician. He was a good composer. Inayat Khan Rasikh has also given the description of a musician called Sheikh Moinuddin, but that description is quite different from the description of Ghulam Mohiuddin.

Sawaad Khan Dhadhi

He was a popular musician and his compositions were also of good quality. He was a resident of Jhunjhunu in Fatehpur, and he died in his home town.[2]

Kishan Khan Kalawant

In some of the manuscripts his name has been written as Kun Khan. Earlier, he was with Shahjahan, but Shah Shuja requested Shahjahan to lend his sevrices for him. He had a good command on Margi Ragas. He died in Bengal.[3]

Wali Dhadhi

He was a commendable singer who died at Akbarabad when he was eighty years old.

Salim Chand Dagar

He was an accomplished singer and some of his compositions are of good standard.[4]

Sheikh Sadullah Lahori

His singing was of a very high standard, and he had a number of disciples. He was very close to Faqueerullah, and at that time he was sixty years old. He was an opium addict which damaged his voice in his old age.[5]

Mohammad Baaqui

He was alive when Faqueerullah wrote his book. His

1. Ibid., p. 97.
2. Ibid., p. 98.
3. Ibid., p. 98.
4. Ibid., p. 98.
5. Ibid., p. 99.

compositions were of good standard but because of regular use of opium his voice was damaged.[1]

Bucha

He was a brother of Sher Mohammad. He was an accomplished musician and his compositions were also of good quality. He died of some chronic disease at the age of fifty six.[2]

Baazeed Khan Nauchhawari

He was also a popular Kalawant who died at the age of fifty six.

Roora Qawwal

He was a very famous Qawwal who died at the age of sixty.

Kabir Qawwal

He was a disciple of Sheikh Sher Mohammad and was alive during the time of Aurangzeb. Faqueerullah praised him and wished him a long life.

Tulsi Ram

He was a Kalawant who died at the age of sixty.

Dharam Das Kalawant

He was a well known musician of his time, whose singing had become defective in his old age. He settled in Agra after leaving his service.

Rahim Khan Dhadhi

His compositions were of good quality. He had some familiarity with the Margi sangeet.[3]

Kavi Jot Dhadhi

He was also an accomplished composer. He died at the age of eighty in his home town Fallor.[4]

Idul Singh

Idul Singh was the son of Raja Ram Shah, the governor of Kharagpur. He used to sing Khayal and Tarana and also composed several songs in these styles.

Mir Ammad

He belonged to Herat. He was a vocalist of high standard.

1. Ibid.
2. Ibid., p. 99.
3. Ibid., p. 100.
4. Ibid.

Hamir Sen and his Son Subal Sen

Both were renowned Kalawants during Aurangzeb's period. Hamir Sen was alive during the time of Akbar also. He died at the age of eighty and Subal Sen died at the age of fifty.

Syed Khan Nohar

Syed Khan was the grandson of Sujan Khan. He was mainly a Dhruvapad singer.

Syed Tayyab

He belonged to a place known as Jharsa and his pseudonym wag Madhu. He had exceptional abilities for music compositions. But his voice was not of good quality. He died at the age of fifty in Agra.

Sunder Ghan (Sudarshan)

He was an average singer, but was good in compositions. He died at the age of seventy.

Wazeer Khan Nauhar

He was a competent singer of Dhruvapad or Geet aad he was also familiar with Amir Khusrau's innovations.[1] Following is the list of instrumentalists as described in Raag Darpan :[2] (1) Saras (2) Bayzeed Rebabi (3) Shikhar Sen (Rebab player) (4) Saleh Dhadhi (Rebab player) (5) Mridang Rai Kirpai (Mridang player) (6) Firoz Dhadhi (Pakhawaj player) (7) Amanullah (Pakhawaj player) (8) Ilahdad Dhadhi (Sarangi player) (9) Tahir Dhadhi (Daff player) (10) Mohammad Ras Bin (Bin player) (11) Shauqui (Tamboor player) (12) Abul Wafa (Tamboor player) (13) Surdas (Pakhawaj player) (14) Surna player (his name has not been mentioned).

So far we have described the musicians belonging to the seventeenth and early eighteenth centuries, whose names are associated with the period of emperors Akbar, Jahangir, Shahjahan and Aurangzeb. This was the period during which there was generally political stability, economic affluence and social harmony. The peace of mind, patronage of the court and aristocrats, and the social status enjoyed by the musicians provided an ideal environment for the development of music and attainment of a high level of excellence by the musicians.

1. Faqueerullah : Raag Darpan;p. 102.
2. Ibid., pp. 102-103.

The situation began to change during Aurangzeb's time and deteriorated rapidly after him. Political instability, intrigues in the court, quick change of the kings, and plunder of the country by invaders like Nadirshah changed the scene which must have created a sense of insecurity among the musicians. This was probably the reason why the musicians started leaving the centre and moved to smaller states. The momentum of earlier traditions seems to have continued until Aurangzeb's time, and that is why we find a number of distinguished names of musicians in the litereture of that period. However, as stated earlier, music had become highly popular and an integral part of social life and culture. Therefore, the popularity of music did not decline. Among the later Mughals the name of Mohammad Shah Rangila (1719-1748 A.D.) is well known for his love for and obsession with music. A detailed description of the musicians of this period is found in Muraqqa-e-Dehli,[1] which was written by Dargah Quli Khan of Hyderabad, who visited Delhi in 1738 A.D. This was the time when Nadirshah had invaded Delhi. Following is a selective description of the musicians from the book written by Dargah Quli Khan :

Nemat Khan

He was the son of Parmol Khan. According to Dargah Quli Khan : "His presence in north India is God's great gift. He is matchless in the art of music. He has a remarkable capacity for composing various styles of songs. At present he is considered the master of contemporary musicians. He does not concede to anybody's request for singing except the King. His supreme proficiency in playing Bin shows that no such Binkar was ever born before him. He has a magic in his voice. He goes to the Dargahs of saints and sometimes also holds musical sittings at his place, where it appears as if the whole of Delhi is thronging".[2]

According to Miraat-e-Aftab-Numa, Nemat Khan used to compose Dhruvapad, Khayal, Tarana and other styles with great maturity, freshness and colourfulness. He acquired

1. This book was translated into Urdu by Khwaja Hasan Nizami, Delhi, 1933.

2. See Nizami, K.H : Purani Dehli Ke Halaat.

the art of music from a Tatari Qawwal, Bengali Natwar and Devdatta Kavishvar. He was honoured and respected in the court of Jahandarshah. King Mohammad Shah brought him up and was his great admirer. Nemat Khan died in the later part of Mohammad Shah's rule.[1]

Accordidg to Inayat Khan Rasikh Nemat Khan from his childhood, used to attend the musical gathering of Mohammad Azam Shah, along with his father Nirmol Khan. In such gatherings he got inspiration from Tatari Qawwal Lala Bangali Natwar and Devdatta Kavishvar. Mohammad Moizuddin Bahadurshah also held him in high esteem. For sometime he lived under the patronage of Qutb-ul-Mulk also. He was an incomprable musician of his time.

A notable point here is that in the literature cited above nowhere the title Sadarang has been mentioned with his name. It appears that this title was associated with the name of Nemat Khan, in the later years of his life, probably during the time of Mohammad Shah Rangila. It is evidently due to this reason that in his compositions which are known even today, his title Sadarang appears; and the compositions include the name of his patron Mohammad Shah Rangila.

Firoze Khan

His title was Adarang. He was the disciple, nephew and son-in-law of Nemat Khan. He was also trained in the same manner as Nemat Khan. He had composed a number of songs which are known even today.[2]

Khusrau Khan

He was the younger brother of Nemat Khan and was a very famous and talented musician. One of his specialities was that he could play a particular type of instrument for a very long duration in different ways. He possessed an instrument with three strings, which was unusual at that time. On that instrument he could play all Raags and Raginis. Possibly this instrument could be the forerunner of the modern instrument sitar. He had also innovated a number of new Raags and Raginis.[3]

1. Arshi, I.A : Hindustan Ke Chand Mashhoor, Mousiqaar Aaj Kal, Aug., 1956.
2. See Nizami, K.H : Purani Dehli Ke Halaat.
3. Ibid.

Taj Khan

He was a very famous Qawwal. His voice was very captivating. He was a devotee of the Sufi saints and was a Sufi himself. He had a prominent position among the musicians of his time.[1]

Jaani and Ghulam Rasul

Both of them were Taaj Khan's sons. They also performed Qawwali, and people were very fond of listening to them. Usually they sang together.

Rahim and Tansen

They were the descendants of Tansen. They were highly admired by the musicians and artistes of his time. They were the masters of singing Dhruvapad and Kavitt.[2]

Qasim Ali

Qasim Ali was one of the bright and talented disciples of Nemat Khan. Having discovered his potential Nemat Khan instructed him with great concern and care. At his young age he was ahead of many well known musicians of his time.

Moinuddin Qawwal

He was pre-eminent among Qawwals; and was regarded by the people as a master among musicians. He had a unique voice which was especially suited to Qawwali.

Burhani Qawwal

He was also an accomplished Qawwal. He possessed a high degree of maturity and perfection in his singing as a result of rigourous practice.[3]

Sawaad Khan

He was considered highly talented and knowledgeable. He was admired by the young artistes of his time and they used to go to seek his guidance.

Shah Daniyaal

Shah Daniyal was a very well known musician. He was regarded an expert of singing Khayal and Kavitt. He was a Sufi and he used to preside over the musical gatherings. In addition to being a good musician he was known for his sense of humour and wit, and his interesting way of describing stories and chutkalas.

1. Ibid.
2. Ibid.
3. Ibid.

Jatta Qawwal

He was a famous Qawwal who used to convey religious message through his Qawwali. He played a prominent role in the gatherings of Sufis. He used to recite verses from Quran with intense feeling and touching melody. He had memorized a large collection of Qauls of old Sufis. He was dear to all the Sufis of Delhi and was serving Shah Basat. He was matchless in his art, during his time. Along with his singing he could play some musical instruments also.[1]

Allah Bande

He was the son of a very famous Qawwal and was a famous Khayal singer. His singing was colourful and melodius.

Panna Bai

She was one of the famous disciples of Nemat Khan Binkar. She had a unique way of singing Tanas, and her Tanas bewildered the audience. She also innovated new Raags, and Raginis. She was invited to almost all the important musical gatherings of Delhi.

Kamaal Bai

Kamaal Bai was a well known musician and dancer. She was given considerable importance in the royal musical gatherings of Mohammad Shah. She used to follow the norms of the classical music carefully, usually she sang Nemat Khan's compositions in which the name of Mohammad Shah was included.

Uma Bai

She was a good singer who used to sing Kavitt and Khayal.

Lal Kanwar

She was the daughter of Uma Bai and beloved of Mohammad Shah. She used to attend the royal musical gatherings regularly.

The Blind Musician

He had acquired a unique skill of playing on his belly like Pakhawaj and Dholak. He was able to play Talas which could be played on Pakhawaj and Dholak. He used to provide effective accompaniment to the women dancers. His belly had become black due to repeated striking.

1. Ibid.

Ghulam Mohammad

He was a renowned Sarangi player whose fame reached distant parts of the country. He played the Raags full of Karuna Ras beautifully. He was an incomparable Sarangi player of his time.

Baqar Tamboorchi

Baqar was a master player of Tamboora of his time. The emperor admired him and he was a highly respected artiste among the music lovers.

Ghasiram Pakhawaji

He was a highly proficient Pakhawaj player and regarded as an eminent musician, among his contemporary Pakhawaj players.

Besides the above mentioned musicians, names and details of a number of other musicians belonging to the eighteenth century have been given by Dargah Quli Khan in his book Muraqqa-e-Dehli. Names of such musicians are being given here : 1. Amir Khan Burhani—(Qawwali and Khayal singer) 2. Rahim Khan Jahani—(Khayal singer) 3. Shujaat Khan—(Geet and Kavitt singer) 4. Ibrahim Khan—(Vocalist) 5. Boley Khan—(Vocalist) 6. Baqar Tamboorchi—(Tamboora player) 7. Hasan Khan—(Rebab player) 8. Hussain Khan—(Dholak player) 9. Thanna—(Dholak player) 10. Shahbaz—(Dhamdhami player) 11. Shah Durvesh—(Blind musician who played Matka) 12. Taqui—(Instrumentalist) 13. Khawasi and Anutha—(Khayal singers and dancers) 14. Sabzah and Mazah—(Dancers) 15. Yaari—(Naqqal) 16. Beloved of Abul Hasan (Khayal singer and dancer) 17. Allah Bande—(Khayal singer) 18. Razi—(Khayal singer) 19. Heenga—(Dancer) 20. Sultana—(Dancer) 21. Dargahi—(Manjeera player) 22. Saras Roop—(Dancer) 23. Noor Bai—(Vocalist) 24. Chamni—(Vocalist) 25. Umar Begum—(Dancer) 26. Maniya—(Dancer) 27. Ramzani—(Vocalist and dancer) 28. Maani Chakmak—(Vocalist) 29. Kaley Kanka—(Dancer) 30. Zeenat and Bhajji—(Vocalists and dancers) 31. Gulab—(Vocalist) 32. Rehman Bai—(Dancer) 33. Ramzaani—(Vocalist) 34. Panna and Tanno—(Vocalists and dancers).

The foregoing discussion and description of the musicians has been based on Ain-e-Akbari, Raag Darpan, Risala-e-Zikr-e-Mughannian-e-Hindustan, Miraat-e-Aftabnuma and Muraqqa-e-Dehli. It reveals that during the seventeenth and eighteenth centuries, broadly, the musicians were classified into two categories, namely—Kalawants and Qawwals. There was a predominance of Dhruvapad singers (Kalawants) in the seventeenth century, while in the eighteenth century the Qawwali and Khayal singers became more popular and a number of women musicians also came to the forefront. It is noteworthy that the musicians generally composed songs and innovated Raags and such creative contributions were highly valued and admired at that time.

Another significant information found in this chapter is that a number of musicians in the seventeenth century were well familiar with the system of Margi-Sangeet, although such music was not performed during those days. Thus Margi had not disappeared until the seventeenth century.

An analysis of the information given in this chapter indicates that during the seventeenth century the orientation of musicians was more towards spiritual aspects and development of the art of music for its own sake whereas in the eighteenth century the orientation changed increasingly towards entertainment and pleasure.

Bibliography

Books (English)

Abul Fazl Allami, Akbar Nama, 3 Vols. Tr. H. Beveridge, Calcutta, 1897-1921.

Ahmad, Aziz, Studies in Islamic Culture in the Indian Environment, Reprint, Oxford, 1966.

Ahmad, Khwaja Nizamuddin, Tabqat-e-Akbari, tr. B. De, Calcutta, 1913-36.

Ali, A. Yusuf, Medieval India, London, 1932.

Athar Ali, M., The Mughal Nobility under Aurangzeb, Bombay, 1956.

Babur Nama, Translated by Annett and Susannah Beveridge, Oriental Books Reprint Corporation, New Delhi, Reprinted 1970

Babur, Zahiruddin Muhammad, Tuzuk-e-Beburi, tr. from Turki Text, A.S. Beveridge, London, 1921.

Badauni, Abdul Qadir, Muntakhab-ut-Twarikh, tr. Vol. I, G.S.A. Ranking, Calcutta, 1895-99 ; Vol. II, W.H. Lowe, 1894-98 ; Vol. III, T.W. Haig, 1895-1925.

Bernier, Francis, Travels in the Mughal Empire, 1656-68, tr. A. Constable, revised by V. A. Smith, 2nd ed., London, 1916.

Bhatkhande, V.N., A Short Historical Survey of the Music of Upper India, Ramachandra Sangeetalaya, Gwalior, 1934.

Blox, Eric Groves, Dictionary of Music & Musicians, Vol. I, IV, Macmillan & Co. Ltd., New York, 1954.

Danielou, A., The Raags of Northern Indian Music, Barrie Rockliff, 2 elements Inn., London, 1968.

Danielou, A., Northern Indian Music, Vol. II, Haleyon Press, London, 1954.

Deva, B.C., Indian Music, Indian Council for Cultural Relations, 1974.

De Laet, Joannes, The Empire of the Great Mogol, tr., J.S. Hoyland, annotated by S.N. Banerjee, Reprint, New Delhi, 1974.

Elliot, H.M., The History of India as Told by its Own Historians, ed., S. Dowson, 8 Vols., London, 1866-77.

Faruqi, M., Aurangzeb and His Times, Bombay, 1935.

Foster, W., Early Travels in India, 1583-1619, London, 1927.

Ganguli, O.C., Raags and Raginis, Munshiram Manoharlal, New Delhi, 1948.

Garret, J., A Classical Dictionary of India, Reprint, Oriental Publishers, New Delhi.

Goswami, O., The Story of Indian Music, Asia Publishing House, New Delhi, 1957.

Gulbadan Begum, Humayun Nama, tr. A.S. Beveridge, London, 1902.

Holroyde, P., Music of India, Praeger Publishers, New York, Washington, 1972.

Irvine, W., Jean de., Later Mughals, Reprint, New Delhi, 1971.

Jahangir, Tuzuk-e-Jahangiri, tr. Alexander & H. Beveridge, Reprint, Delhi, 1968.

Jairazbhoy, N.A., The Raags of North Indian Music, Faber and Faber, London, 1971.

Jones, W., Music of India, Anil Gupta, Calcutta (revised ed.), 1962.

Khan, Yusuf Hussain, Medieval Indian Culture, Bombay, 1959.

Manucci, Niccolao, Storia Do Mogor, tr. W. Irvine, 4 Vols. London, 1907-08.

Pandey, A.B., Later Medieval India, Central Book Depot, Allahabad, 1963.

Popley, H.A., The Music of India, Y.M.C.A., Calcutta, 1921, Revised, 1950.

Prajnananda, A Historical Study of Indian Music, Ananddhara Prakashan, Calcutta, 1965.

———————.Music of the Nations (A Comparative Study), Munshiram Manoharlal, 1973.

Prasad, Beni, History of Jahangir, 3rd ed., Allahabad, 1940.

Ranade, G.H., Hindusthani Music, Popular Prakashan Bombay, 1939.

Rangacharya, A., Introduction to Bharata's Natya Shastra, Popular Prakashan, Bombay, 1966.

Rushbrook, William, L.F., An Empire Builder of the Sixteenth Century, London, 1918.

Saksena, B.P., History of Shahjahan of Delhi, Allahabad 1940.

Sambamoorty, L. History of Indian Music,Indian Music Publishing House, Madras, 1960.

Sarkar, J.N., History of Aurangzeb, Calcutta, (5 Vols. 1925-34).

Sarkar, J.N., Fall of the Mughal Empire, Calcutta, (4 Vols. 1932-1935.

———.Anecdotes of Aurangzeb, Calcutta, 4th ed., 1963.

Steiggas, F., Persian-English Dictionary, Reprint, New Delhi, 1973.

Srivastava, A.L., The Mughal Empire, Shiv Lal Agarwal and Co., Agra, seventh edition, 1970.

Strangeways, F., Music of Hindustan, Oriental Books, Reprint Corporation, New Delhi, 1975.

Tagore, S.M., Universal History of Music, Varanasi, second edition, 1963.

Tara Chand, Influence of Islam on Indian Culture, 2nd edition, Allahabad, 1963.

Tarlekar, G.H., Studies in the Natya Shastra, Motilal Banarsi Das, New Delhi, 1975.

Tomas, W.F., Mutual Influence of Muhammadans and Hindus in India, Cambridge, 1892.

Travenier, J.B., Travels in India, 1640-47, tr, V. Ball, revised by W. Crooke, London, 1925.

Tyulayesj, Miniatures of Babur Nama, Moscow, 1960.

Willard, N.A., Music of India, Anil Gupta P. Ltd., Calcutta, rev. ed., 1962.

Articles (English)

Chowdhry, B.C.R., 'Revival of Dhruvapad' Lakshya Sangeet, Sept., 1958.

Maudgalya, V.C., 'Evolution of Khayal' Synopsis of illustrated talk, Indian Music Journal, 1971.

Mutatkar, S., 'Evolution of Indian Music' (a series of special articles and papers read at the Symposium arranged by All India Radio)

———'Some Aspects of Dhruvapad' (illustrated talk).

———'Evolution of Indian Music' Lakshya Sangeet, Jun., 1956.

Sharma, P.L., 'The Thumri', Indian Music Journal, Oct.-Nov., 1966.

———.'Synopsis of Treatise Shahasrasa', Indian Music Journal, Vol. VIII-IX-X.

Singh, J.S., 'The Evolution of Khayal' (Commemoration Volume in Honour of Dr. S.N. Ratanjankar, 1961).

Books (Hindi)

Ahmad, N., Kitab-e-Nauras (introduction in English) Bharatiya Kala Kendra, New Delhi, 1956.

Ahmad, S.I., Sharqui Rajya Jaunpur Ka Itihas, Shiraz Prakashan Bhawan, Jaunpur, 1968.

Ali, R.N., Maarifun-Naghmat (translation) Sangeet Karyalaya, Hathras, Second edition, 1958.

Bhatkhande, V.N., Bhatkhande Sangeet Shastra (4 vols.) Sangeet Karyalay, Hathras, 1951.

———.Sangeet Granth, Commemoration Volume, Indira Kala Sangeet Vishvavidyalaya, Khairagarh (MP). 1966.

Brihaspati, K.C.D. Mussalman Aur Bharatiya Sangeet, Rajkamal Prakashan, Delhi, 1974.

Brihaspati, Dhruvapad Aur Us Ka Vikas, Bihar Rashtrabhasha Parishad, 1951.

Garg, L.N., Nibandha Sangeet (compilation), Sangeet Karyalaya, Hathras, 1978.

Gupta, V., Adhunik Pragati Kavya Mein Sangitatva, Nagri Pracharini Sabha, Varanasi, 1970.

Paranjape, S.S., Bharatiya Sangeet Ka Itihas, Chaukhamba Sanskrit Series, Varanasi, 1969.

Rizvi, A.A., Mughal Kaleen Bharat, Aligarh.

Sharma, P.L., Sahasrasa (edited), Sangeet Natak Academy, New Delhi, 1972.

Articles (Hindi)

Anandpal Singh, S., Dhruvapad Ke Sambandh mein Bhatkhande Ji ke Vichar', Sangeet, May, 1966.

Awasthi, 'Dhruvapad Aur Uske Uday Kaal Ki Paristhitiyan' Sangeet Kala Vihar, 1977.

Brihaspati, K.C.D., 'Qawwali : Ek Bharatiya Shaili, Jan.-Feb., 1979.

———.'Bharatiya Sangeet Ke Param Bhakt Amir Khursau, Sangeet, Jan.-Feb., 1976.

Brihaspati, K.C.D. 'Bharatiya Sangeet Ke Param Bhakt Sangeet, Apr., 1968.

Brihaspati, K.C.D. 'Dhamar Gayaki : Ek Rangarang Parampara Sangeet, Apr., 1968.

Devangan, T.S. 'Tarana : Ek Vishleshnatmak Drishti', Sangeet, Tarana Ank, 1968.

Ginde, K.R., 'Dhruvapad', Lakshya Sangeet, Mar., 1957.

Goswami, P.C. 'Qawwali Katha', Sangeet, Jul., 1979.

Khan, C., 'Tarana Gayaki Ki Kuchh Visheshtayen', Sangeet, Jan., 1968.

Madhukar, K.L., 'Khayal Gayaki Par Ek Drishti', Sangeet, Jan.-Feb., 1976.

Rasul, G., 'Sada Bahar Gayan Shaili : Tarana', Sangeet, Jan-Feb., 1968.

Ratanjankar, S.N. 'Dhruvapad Gayaki Ki Samasyayen', Lakshya Sangeet, Jan.-Feb., 1958.

Sharma, K. 'Thumri, Udgam aur Vikas', Sangeet Kala Vihar, Aug., 1956.

Singh, S.B. 'Khayali Duniya Ki Upaj Khayal,' Sangeet, May, 1965.

Manuscripts and Books (Persian)

Abul Fazl Allami, Akbar Nama, 3 Vols., Calcutta, 1873-87.

Ahmad, K.N. Tabqat-e-Akbari, 3 Vols., Calcutta, 1913, 1927, 1931.

Badauni, A.Q., Muntakhab-ut-Tawarikh, 3 Vols. Calcutta, 1864, 1868.

Faqueerullah, Amir, Raag Darpan (manuscript), Dr. Zakir Husain Library, Jamia Millia Islamia, New Delhi.

Firishta, M.Q. Hindushah, Gulshan-e-Ibrahimi, Lucknow. n.d.I.

Jahangir, Tuzuk-e-Jahangiri, 3 Vols., Ghazipur and Aligarh, 1863-64.

Kazim, Mohammad, Alamgir Nama, Calcutta, 1865-73.

Khafi Khan, M.H., Muntakhabul-Lubab, 3 Vols. Calcutta, 1860-74, 1900-1925.

Khwand, Amir, Humayun Nama, Calcutta, 1940.

Lahauri, A.H., Badshah Nama, 2 Vols., Calcutta, 1866-72.

Lodi, S.K. Miraatul-Khayal, Calcutta, 1831.

Miraat-e-Aftab Numa, (manuscript), India Office Library, London, Reza Library, Rampur.

Mutmad Khan, Iqbal Nama-e-Jahangiri, 3 Vols., Lucknow, 1870.

Mustaid Khan, Muhammad Saqi, Maasir-e-Alamgiri, Calcutta, 1870-73.

Naghmat-e-Sarod (manuscript), Faculty of Music and Fine Arts, University of Delhi.

Parijatak (manuscript), tr. of Sanskrit book Sangeet Parijat of Ahobal, Maulana Azad Library, Aligarh Muslim University.

Raag Darpan (manuscript), Dr. Zakir Husain Library, Jamia Millia Islamia, New Delhi.

Rasikh, I.K. Risala-e-Zikr-e-Mughannian-e-Hindustan, ed. by S. Haider, Department of Arabic and Persian, Patna University, 1961.

Sarmadi, Shahab, Ghunyatul-Munya (edited), Asia Publishing House Pvt. Ltd., New Delhi, 1971.

Sautun Nuqush, Nawal Kishore Press, Lucknow, 1884.

Shah Nawaz Khan, Maasirul-Umara, Calcutta, 1888-91.

Tashrihul-Mousiqi (manuscript). Shirani Collection, Punjab University, Lahore.

Tohfat-ul-Hind, ed. by N.H. Ansari, published in Iran, 1950.

Tohfat-ul-Hind (manuscript).

Usulun-Naghmat-e-Asifi (manuscript), Dr. Zakir Husain Library, Jamia Millia Islamia, New Delhi.

Books and Articles (Urdu)

Alam S., Nadirat-e-Shahi (manuscript), Reza Library, Rampur.

Ansari, N.H., Farsi Adab ba-Ahde-Aurangzeb, Delhi, 1969.

Arshi, I.A., 'Hindustan Ke Chand Mashhoor Mousiqaar' (article), Aaaj Kal, Aug., 1956.

————.Nadirat-e-Shahi (edited) Reza Library, Rampur.

Haideri, A., Irfan-e-Mousiqi, Kutub Khana-e-Anjuman, Taraqqi-e-Urdu Board, New Delhi.

Imam, M.K. Madanul-Mousiqi, Hindustani Press; Lucknow, 1925.

Jafri, R.A., Wajid Ali Shah aur unka Ahd, Kitab Manzil, Lucknow.

Khan, Chand, Mousiqi Hazrat Amir Khusrau, Mousiqi Book Depot, Delhi, 1978.

Khan, N.M., Hayat-e-Amir Khusrau, Sheikh Ghulam and

Sons Publishers, Lahore.

Kanwal, S., 'Ilm-e-Mousiqi' (article), Aaaj Kal, Aug., 1956.

Malik R., Hazrat Amir Khusrau Ka Ilm-e-Mousiqi Aur Doosre Maqalaat, Karachi.

Nizami, K.H., Purani Dehli Ke Halaat, tr. of Dargah Quli Khan.

Rizvi, M.H., Lakhnau Ka Shahi Stage, Tanzeem Press, Lucknow, 1957.

Books (Sanskrit)

Sangeet Makrand, ed. with introduction and appendices by Mangesh Ramakrishna Telang, published under the authority of the Government of His Highness, The Maharaja Gaekwad of Baroda, 1920.

Sangeet Raj, ed. by P.L. Sharma, Hindu Vishva Vidyalaya, Sanskrit Publication Board, Banaras.

Sangeet Ratnakar, Hindi tr. by Suresh Chandra Bandopadhyay, Calcutta.

Sarangdeva, Sangeet Ratnakara, ed. by Pt. S. Shastri, The Adyar Library and Research Centre, Madras, first edition, 1944.